BASIC DOCUMENTS
IN CANADIAN HISTORY

JAMES J. TALMAN

Chief Librarian and Professor
Faculty of Graduate Studies
The University of Western Ontario

AN ANVIL ORIGINAL

under the general editorship of

LOUIS L. SNYDER

D. VAN NOSTRAND COMPANY, INC.

PRINCETON, NEW JERSEY

TORONTO   LONDON

NEW YORK

To

Liv Elizabeth
and
John Davis

FC
16
.T3
1959 / 58,132

D. VAN NOSTRAND COMPANY, INC.

120 Alexander St., Princeton, New Jersey (*Principal office*)
257 Fourth Avenue, New York 10, New York
25 Hollinger Rd., Toronto 16, Canada
358, Kensington High Street, London, W.14, England

PREFACE

THE purpose of this volume is to provide a selection of documents to illustrate the development of Canada from an unexplored geographical region to an independent world power. The framework is constitutional because political unification and autonomy were requisite before Canada could gain the position she has achieved in the world today. Moreover, Canada led the way in breaking away, by peaceful means, from colonial dependence on Great Britain, thereby setting the pattern by which the British Commonwealth of Nations has evolved. These achievements were not accidental, and the vision of leading proponents of Canadian nationhood is revealed in their pronouncements printed here.

A major influence on Canada's development has been her relationship with the United States. The peaceful coexistence and close ties between Canada and the United States, not unmarred by misunderstanding, have been indicated by several documents.

Since the greatest development of Canada came in the twentieth century nineteen of the fifty-two documents belong to this century.

I am indebted to Miss Julia Jarvis, Secretary of the Champlain Society, Mr. Pierre Brunet, Acting Dominion Archivist, and Professor John T. Saywell, Editor of *The Canadian Historical Review,* for giving me *carte blanche* to use any document published by their respective bodies. In addition, I must thank Dr. C. Bruce Fergusson, Provincial Archivist of Nova Scotia, for supplying the account of the arrival of the *Britannia* at Halifax in 1840; Professor Gordon O. Rothney, of Memorial University, St. John's Newfoundland, for advice and assistance with the history of Newfoundland, about which comparatively little has been written; Miss Ruth Buggey, Librarian of the *Winnipeg Free Press* for supplying, and Col. Clifford Sifton D.S.O., and Dr. Victor Sifton for permission to use, the 1925 speech of Sir Clifford Sifton; and Mr. H. O.

White, M.P. and the Department of External Affairs for supplying the not too readily available agreement to establish the Commonwealth Air Training Plan.

I am grateful to my colleagues in the Library and History Department of the University of Western Ontario, who were generous with time and advice on what documents to include. In the end, however, the decision on what or what not to include had to rest with the editor, who must assume full responsibility.

Finally, I must record my indebtedness to my wife for her interest and invaluable assistance in preparing the manuscript.

London, Canada   JAMES J. TALMAN
February 1959

TABLE OF CONTENTS

— 1 —

JACQUES CARTIER SAILS UP THE ST. LAWRENCE, 1535[1]

Jacques Cartier was born in the seaport of St. Malo, Brittany, France, in 1491. Little is known of his early history as a mariner until he appears as pilot of an expedition to America in 1534. His first voyage took him to Newfoundland, Labrador, and the Gulf of St. Lawrence. The second voyage, made in 1535 and 1536, is more significant than the first because Cartier penetrated to Stadacona (Quebec) and Hochelaga (Montreal). He returned to Canada in 1541, but little is known of this voyage. The extract given here from the narrative of the second voyage describes Cartier's arrival at Stadacona and Hochelaga.

✓ ✓ ✓

. . . On [Tuesday], the seventh of the month [September, 1535], being our Lady's day, after hearing mass, we set out from this [Coudres] island to proceed up stream, and came to fourteen islands which lay some seven or eight leagues beyond Coudres island. This is the point where the province and territory of Canada begins. One of these islands is large, being some ten leagues long and five leagues wide, and is inhabited by Indians who are much employed in fishing for the many varieties of fish caught in this river, according to the season. Mention will be made of these fish farther on. After we had cast

[1] H. P. Biggar, "The Voyages of Jacques Cartier," *Publications of the Public Archives of Canada,* No. 11 (Ottawa, 1924), 119-124, 149-156.

anchor between this large island and the north shore, we went on land and took with us the two Indians we had seized on our former voyage. We came upon several of the people of the country who began to run away and would not come near, until our two Indians had spoken to them and told them that they were Taignoagny and Dom Agaya. And when they knew who it was, they began to welcome them, dancing and going through many ceremonies. And some of the headmen came to our long-boats, bringing us many eels and other fish, with two or three measures of Indian corn, which is their bread in that country, and many large melons. And during that day many canoes filled with the people of the country, both men as well as women, came to our ships to see and welcome our two Indians. The Captain received them all well and treated them to what he had to offer. And to ingratiate himself with them, he gave them some small presents of little value, at which they were much pleased.

On the morrow, the lord of Canada, named Donnacona (but as chief they call him *Agouhanna*), came to our ships accompanied by many Indians in twelve canoes. He then sent back ten of these and came alongside our ships with only two canoes. And when he was opposite to the smallest of our three ships [*Emérillon*], this *Agouhanna* began to make a speech and to harangue us, moving his body and his limbs in a marvellous manner, as is their custom when showing joy and contentment. And when he came opposite to the Captain's vessel, on board of which were Taignoagny and Dom Agaya, the chief spoke to them and they to him, telling him what they had seen in France, and the good treatment meted out to them there. At this the chief was much pleased and begged the Captain to stretch out his arms to him that he might hug and kiss them, which is the way they welcome one in that country. After this the Captain stepped down into this *Agouhanna's* canoe, and ordered bread and wine to be brought that the chief and his Indians might partake thereof. When this had been done they were much pleased; but no other present was then made to the chief, pending a more suitable time and place. After these things had been thus carried out, they took leave of each other and separated, the said *Agouhanna* returning to his canoes to make his way home again. And the Captain likewise ordered out our long-boats to make our way up the stream with the flood tide, to find a harbour and safe spot in which to lay up the ships. And we went some ten leagues up the river, coasting this island [of Orleans], at the end of which we came to a forking of the waters, which is an exceedingly pleasant spot, where there is a small river and a harbour with a bar, on which at high tide, there is a depth of from two to three fathoms. We thought this river [St. Charles] a suitable place in which to lay up our ships in safety. We named it "Ste. Croix," as we arrived there that day. Near this spot lives a tribe of which this Donnacona is chief, and he himself resides there. The village is called Stadacona. This region is as fine land as it is possible to see, being very fertile and covered with magnificent trees of the same varieties as in France, such as oaks, elms, ash, walnut, plum-trees, yew-trees, cedars, vines, hawthorns, bearing a fruit as large as a damson, and other varieties of trees. Beneath these grows as good hemp as that of France, which comes up without sowing or tilling it.

And we sailed on in as fine weather as one could wish until [Saturday] October 2, [1535] when we arrived at Hochelaga, which is about forty-five leagues from the spot where we had left our bark. During this interval we came across on the way many of the people of the country, who brought us fish and other provisions, at the same time dancing and showing great joy at our coming. And in order to win and keep their friendship, the Captain made them a present of some knives, beads and other small trifles, whereat they were greatly pleased. And on reaching Hochelaga, there came to meet us more than a thousand persons, both men, women and children, who gave us as good a welcome as ever father gave to his son, making great signs of joy; for the men danced in one ring, the women in another and the children also apart by themselves. After this they brought us quantities of fish, and of their bread which is made of Indian corn, throwing so much of it into our long-boats that it seemed to rain bread. Seeing this the Captain, accompanied by several of his men, went on shore; and no sooner had he landed than they all crowded about him and about the

others, giving them a wonderful reception. And the
women brought their babies in their arms to have the
Captain and his companions touch them, while all held a
merry-making which lasted more than half an hour. Seeing their generosity and friendliness, the Captain had the
women all sit down in a row and gave them some tin
beads and other trifles; and to some of the men he gave
knives. Then he returned on board the long-boats to sup
and pass the night, throughout which the Indians remained on the bank of the river, as near the long-boats as
they could get, keeping many fires burning all night, and
dancing and calling out every moment *aguyase* which is
their term of salutation and joy.

How the Captain and the Gentlemen, Accompanied by Twenty-Five Well-Armed and Marshalled Sailors, Went to Visit the Village of Hochelaga; and of the Situation of the Place.

At daybreak the next day, the Captain, having put on
his armour, had his men marshalled for the purpose of
paying a visit to the village and home of these people,
and to a mountain which lies near the town. The Captain
was accompanied by the gentlemen and by twenty sailors,
the remainder having been left behind to guard the long-
boats. And he took three Indians of the village as guides
to conduct them thither. When we had got under way, we
discovered that the path was as well-trodden as it is possible to see, and that the country was the finest and most
excellent one could find anywhere, being everywhere full
of oaks, as beautiful as in any forest in France, under-
neath which the ground lay covered with acorns. And
after marching about a league and a half, we met on the
trail one of the headmen of the village of Hochelaga, accompanied by several Indians, who made signs to us that
we should rest at that spot near a fire they had lighted on
the path; which we did. Thereupon this headman began
to make a speech and to harangue us, which, as before
mentioned, is their way of showing joy and friendliness,
welcoming in this way the Captain and his company. The
Captain presented him with a couple of hatchets and a
couple of knives, as well as with a cross and a crucifix,

which he made him kiss and then hang it about his neck. For these the headman thanked the Captain. When this was done we marched on, and about half a league thence, found that the land began to be cultivated. It was fine land with large fields covered with the corn of the country, which resembles Brazil millet, and is about as large or larger than a pea. They live on this as we do on wheat. And in the middle of these fields is situated and stands the village of Hochelaga, near and adjacent to a mountain, the slopes of which are fertile and are cultivated, and from the top of which one can see for a long distance. We named this mountain "Mount Royal." The village is circular and is completely enclosed by a wooden palisade in three tiers like a pyramid. The top one is built crosswise, the middle one perpendicular and the lowest one of strips of wood placed lengthwise. The whole is well joined and lashed after their manner, and is some two lances in height. There is only one gate and entrance to this village, and that can be barred up. Over this gate and in many places about the enclosure are species of galleries with ladders for mounting to them, which galleries are provided with rocks and stones for the defence and protection of the place. There are some fifty houses in this village, each about fifty or more paces in length, and twelve or fifteen in width, built completely of wood and covered in and bordered up with large pieces of the bark and rind of trees, as broad as a table, which are well and cunningly lashed after their manner. . . .

— 2 —

THE VOYAGES TO THE GREAT RIVER ST. LAWRENCE BY THE SIEUR DE CHAMPLAIN, . . . FROM THE YEAR 1608 UNTIL 1612[2]

Credit for establishing the first permanent settlement in Canada belongs to Samuel de Champlain, "The Father of New France." Born in France in 1567, Champlain made his first voyage to the St. Lawrence region in 1603, and in 1604 he took part with De Monts in an abortive attempt to establish a French colony in Acadia. It was on his third voyage, in 1608, that he succeeded in founding a settlement at Quebec. From his base at Quebec he made further explorations, discovering Lake Champlain and exploring the Ottawa Valley. In 1615 he reached Georgian Bay by way of the Ottawa River and Lake Nipissing. The documents given here describe Champlain's arrival at Quebec, the construction of the first buildings in the settlement, and the difficulties of the first winter.

✓   ✓   ✓

. . . From the island of Orleans to Quebec is one league, and I arrived there on July the third [1608]. On arrival I looked for a place suitable for our settlement, but I could not find any more suitable or better situated than the point of Quebec, so called by the natives, which was covered with nut-trees. I at once employed a part of our workmen in cutting them down to make a site for our settlement, another part in sawing planks, another in dig-

[2] H. P. Biggar, ed., *The Works of Samuel de Champlain* (Toronto, The Champlain Society, 1925), II, 24-25, 35-37, 44-45, 52-53, 59, 63.

ging the cellar and making ditches, and another in going to Tadoussac with the pinnace to fetch our effects. The first thing we made was the storehouse, to put our supplies under cover, and it was promptly finished by the diligence of everyone and the care I took in the matter. . . .

I continued the construction of our quarters, which contained three main buildings of two stories. Each one was three fathoms long and two and a half wide. The storehouse was six long and three wide, with a fine cellar six feet high. All the way round our buildings I had a gallery made, outside the second story, which was a very convenient thing. There were also ditches fifteen feet wide and six deep, and outside these I made several salients which enclosed a part of the buildings, and there we put our cannon. In front of the building there is an open space four fathoms wide and six or seven long, which abuts upon the river's bank. Round about the buildings are very good gardens, and an open place on the north side of a hundred, or a hundred and twenty, yards long and fifty or sixty wide. Nearer Quebec there is a little river [St. Charles], which comes from a lake in the interior, distant six or seven leagues from our settlement. I consider that in this river, which is north a quarter north-west of our settlement, was the place where Jacques Cartier passed the winter; since at a league's distance up this river are still the remains as of a chimney, whose foundation we discovered, and to all appearance what seem to have been ditches about his house, which was small. We found also large, squared, worm-eaten pieces of wood, and some three or four cannon-balls. All these things show clearly that this was a settlement which was founded by Christians. And what makes me say and think that it was Jacques Cartier, is the fact that there is no evidence that anyone wintered or put up buildings there, except Jacques Cartier at the time of his explorations. . . .

Whilst the carpenters, sawyers, and other workmen were busy at our quarters, I set all the rest to work clearing the land about our settlement in order to make gardens in which to sow grains and seed, for the purpose of seeing how the whole thing would succeed, particularly since the soil seemed to be very good.

Meanwhile many of the natives had encamped near us, who used to fish for eels, which begin to come up about September 15 and finish on October 15. During this time the natives all live upon this manna and dry some for the winter to last till the month of February, when the snow is two and a half or even three feet deep at the most. At that time when their eels and the other things which they dry are prepared, they go off beaver-hunting and remain away until the beginning of January. When they were engaged on this, they left in our keeping all their eels and other things till their return, which took place on December 15. And they told us that they did not take many beavers because the waters were too high, on account of the rivers overflowing. I gave them back all their provisions which only lasted them till January 20. When their eels give out they resort to hunting the moose and any other wild beasts they may find, until springtime, at which season I was able to furnish them with various supplies. I studied their customs very particularly. . . .

On the first of October I had some wheat sown and on the fifteenth some rye. On the third of the month there was a white frost and on the fifteenth the leaves of the trees began to fall. On the twenty-fourth of the month I had some native vines planted and they prospered extremely well, but after I left the settlement to come back to France, they were all ruined, for want of care, which distressed me very much.

On the eighteenth of November there was a heavy fall of snow. It lay on the ground only two days, but during that time there was a great gale. During that month there died of dysentery a sailor and our locksmith, as well as several natives on account, in my opinion, of having eaten badly-cooked eels.

On the fifth of February it snowed hard and there was a high wind which lasted for two days. . . .

The scurvy began very late, that is in February, and lasted till the middle of April. Eighteen were struck down with it and of these ten died: and five others died of dysentery. I had some of them opened to see if they were affected like those I had seen in the other settlements. The same conditions were found. Some time after our surgeon died. All this gave us much trouble, on account of the difficulty we had in nursing the sick. . . .

On the fifth of June there arrived at our settlement a shallop, in which was the Sieur des Marais, Pont-Gravé's son-in-law, who brought us news of the arrival of his father-in-law at Tadoussac on the twenty-eighth of May. This gave me much satisfaction; for we hoped to have relief from him. Of our company now only eight of the twenty-eight remained and half of these were ailing. . . .

— 3 —

KING CHARLES'S COMMISSION FOR THE WELL GOVERNING OF HIS SUBJECTS INHABITING NEWFOUNDLAND, OR TRAFFICKING IN BAYS, CREEKS, OR FRESH RIVERS THERE, FEBRUARY 10, 1634[3]

Although Newfoundland appears to have been well known for many years before the ill-fated expedition of Sir Humphrey Gilbert in 1583, settlement was slow. Gilbert, contrary to a widely perpetuated myth, did not formally take possession of the island. He declared Elizabethan sovereignty for a certain number of miles in every direction from St. John's, but this was simply a device to

[3] Lewis Amadeus Anspach, *A History of the Island of Newfoundland* (London, 1819), 498-503. Also printed in *In the Matter of the Boundary between the Dominion of Canada and the Colony of Newfoundland in the Labrador Peninsula* (London, n.d.), IV of joint appendix, 1719-1722.

legalize the taxation, virtually the robbery, of vessels of all nations which he found in that island. When he left, things went on in Newfoundland as they had before his arrival. The charter given here aimed to protect the fishermen from England at the expense of those who lived in Newfoundland. It is called the "Western Charter" because it was advantageous to the fishermen from the West Country of England—Dorset, Devon, Somerset, and Cornwall. The captain of the first ship to reach a harbor each spring became "admiral" of the harbor for that season. These rulers were called "fishing admirals." Their powers existed theoretically at least until the French revolutionary wars, when English fishermen ceased to come to the coasts of Newfoundland. The charter is important because its provisions held back the development of Newfoundland, which was not recognized as a "normal" colony until 1824.

✠   ✠   ✠

Charles, by the Grace of God, King of England, Scotland, France, and Ireland, Defender of the Faith, and so forth, to all to whom these presents shall come, greeting.

Whereas, the region or country, called Newfoundland, hath been acquired to the dominion of our progenitors, which we hold, and our people have many years resorted to those parts, where, and on the coasts adjoining, they employed themselves in fishing, whereby a great number of our people have been set on work, and the navigation and mariners of our realm have been much increased; and our subjects resorting thither, one by the other, and the natives of those parts, were orderly and gently entreated, until of late some of our subjects of the realm of England planting themselves in that country, and there residing and inhabiting, have imagined that for wrongs or injuries done there, either on the shore or in the sea adjoining, they cannot be here impeached; and the rather for that we, or our progenitors, have not hitherto given laws to the inhabitants there, and, by that example, our subjects resorting thither injure one another and use all manner of excess, to the great hindrance of the voyage and common damage of this realm: for preventing such inconveniences hereafter, we do hereby declare in what manner our people in Newfoundland and upon the seas adjoining, and the bays, creeks, and fresh rivers there, shall be guided and governed. . . .

1st. If any man on the land there shall kill another, or if any shall secretly or forcibly steal the goods of any other in the value of forty shillings, he shall be forthwith apprehended and arrested, detained, and brought prisoner into England. . . .

2d. That no ballast, prestones, or any thing else hurtful to the harbours, be thrown out to the prejudice of the said harbours; but that it be carried on shore, and laid where it may not do annoyance.

3d. That no person whatever, either fisherman or in-habitant, do destroy, deface, or any way work any spoil or detriment to any stage, cook-room, flakes, spikes, nails, or any thing else that belongeth to the stages whatsoever, either at the end of the voyage, when he hath done and is to depart the country, or to any such stages as he shall fall withal at his coming into the country; but that he or they content themselves with such stage or stages only as shall be needful for them; and that, for the repairing of such stages as he or they take, they shall fetch timber out of the woods, and not do it with the ruining or tearing of other stages.

4th. That, *according to the ancient custom*, every ship, or fisher that first entereth a harbour in behalf of the ship, be *Admiral* of the said harbour, wherein, for the time being, he shall receive only so much beech and flakes, or both, as is needful for the number of boats that he shall use, with an overplus only for one boat more than he needeth, as a privilege for his first coming;—and that every ship coming after content himself with what he shall have necessary use for, without keeping or detaining any more to the prejudice of others next coming;—and that any that are possessed of several places in several harbours shall be bound to resolve upon which of them they choose, and to send advice to such after-comers in those places, as expect their resolution, and that within eight and forty hours, if the weather so serve, in order that the said aftercomers may likewise choose their places, and so none receive prejudice by others' delay.

5th. That no person cut out, deface, or any way alter or change the marks of any boats or train-fats, whereby to defraud the right owners; and that no person convert to his own use the said boats or train-fats so belonging to others, without their consents; nor remove, nor take them from the places where they be left by the owners, except *in case of necessity;* and then to give notice thereof to the Admiral and others, whereby the right owners may know what is become of them.

6th. That no person do diminish, take away, purloin, or steal any fish, or train, or salt, which is put in casks, train-fats, or cook-room, or other house, in any of the harbours or fishing places of the country, or any other provision belonging to the fishing trade or to the ships.

7th. That no person set fire in any of the woods of the country, or work any detriment or destruction to the same, by *rinding of the trees,* either for the sealing of ships' holds or for rooms on shore, or for any other uses, except for the covering of the roofs for cook-rooms to dress their meat in, and these rooms not to extend above sixteen feet in length at the most.

8th. That no man cast anchor or aught else hurtful, which may breed annoyance, or hinder the haling of seines for bait in places accustomed thereunto.

9th. That no person rob the nets of others out of any drift, boat, or drover for bait, by night, nor take away any bait out of their fishing-boats by their ships' sides, nor rob or steal any of their nets, or any part thereof.

10th. That no person do set up any tavern for selling of wine, beer, or strong waters, cyder, or tobacco, to entertain the fishermen; because it is found that by such means they are debauched, neglecting their labours, and poor ill-governed men not only spend most part of their *shares* before they come home, upon which the life and maintenance of their wives and children depend, but are likewise hurtful in divers other ways, as, by neglecting and making themselves unfit for their labour, by purloining and stealing from their owners, and by making unlawful shifts to supply their disorders, which disorders they frequently follow since these occasions have presented themselves.

Lastly. That, upon the *Sundays* the company assemble

in meet places, and have divine service to be said by some of the masters of the ships, or some others; which prayers shall be such as are in the Book of Common Prayer. , . .

Also, we will and ordain, that these laws and ordinances shall stand in force and be put in due execution until we shall otherwise provide and ordain; and we do require the Admirals in every harbour in this next season ensuing, calling together such as shall be in that harbour, publicly to proclaim these presents, and that they also proclaim the same on shore.

In witness whereof, we have caused these our letters to be made patent.

Witness ourself at Westminster, the 10th day of February, in the ninth year of our reign.

God save the King.
WILLYS

— 4 —

THE ROYAL CHARTER FOR INCOR-PORATING THE HUDSON'S BAY COMPANY, MAY 2, 1670[4]

The incorporation of the Hudson's Bay Company launched English trading activity in the northern parts of Canada. The charter granted extremely wide powers. At first the Company confined its activities to the east shore of Hudson Bay but soon moved to the west shore. As furs became scarce the search went farther and farther

[4] Beckles Willson, *The Great Company* (Toronto, 1899), 515-526. Also printed in *Charters, Statutes, Orders-in-Council, etc. relating to the Hudson's Bay Company* (London, 1931), 3-21.

west until the flag of the Company reached the shores of the Pacific.

After two centuries of existence, the Company in 1870, in return for a payment of £300,000, surrendered certain rights to the Crown, but retained the posts it actually occupied in the North-Western Territory, with certain lands around them. In addition, the Company was given rights to one-twentieth of the lands within the "fertile belt" bounded by the United States boundary, the Rocky Mountains, the northern branch of the Saskatchewan River, and Lake Winnipeg and the Lake of the Woods, as the lands were set out for settlement. Ultimately, the Company received approximately 7,000,000 acres in the present provinces of Manitoba, Saskatchewan, and Alberta. All has been sold except about 6,000 acres.

After almost three centuries, the Company is still an important corporation in Canada. In addition to the fur trade, it has departmental stores in Victoria, Vancouver, Calgary, Edmonton, Saskatoon, and Winnipeg, and many smaller stores. It deals also in land, and has crude oil and natural gas interests.

✓   ✓   ✓

Charles the Second, by the grace of God, King of England, Scotland, France and Ireland, Defender of the Faith, &c.

To all to whom these presents shall come, greeting:

Whereas our dear entirely beloved Cousin, Prince Rupert, Count Palatine of the Rhine, Duke of Bavaria and Cumberland, &c.; Christopher Duke of Albemarle, William Earl of Craven, Henry Lord Arlington, Anthony Lord Ashley, Sir John Robinson, and Sir Robert Vyner, Knights and Baronets; Sir Peter Colleton, Baronet; Sir Edward Hungerford, Knight of the Bath; Sir Paul Neele, Knight; Sir John Griffith and Sir Philip Carteret, Knights; James Hayes, John Kirk, Francis Millington, William Prettyman, John Fenn, Esquires; and John Portman, Citizen and Goldsmith of London; have, at their own great cost, and charges, undertaken an expedition for Hudson's Bay in the north-west part of America, for the discovery of a new passage into the South Sea, and for the finding some trade for furs, minerals, and other considerable commodities, and by such their undertaking have already made such discoveries as to encourage them to proceed further in pursuance of their said design, by means whereof there may probably arise very great advantages to us and our kingdom.

And whereas the said undertakers, for their further encouragement in the said design, have humbly besought us to incorporate them, . . .

Now know ye, that . . . they, and such others as shall be admitted into the said society as is hereafter expressed, shall be one body corporate and politic, in deed and in name, by the name of "The Governor and Company of Adventurers of England trading into Hudson's Bay," . . .

We . . . do give, grant and confirm, unto the said Governor and Company, and their successors, the sole trade and commerce of all these seas, straits, bays, rivers, lakes, creeks and sounds, in whatsoever latitude they shall be, that lie within the entrance of the straits, commonly called Hudson's Straits, together with all the lands and territories upon the countries, coasts, and confines of the seas, bays, lakes, rivers, creeks and sounds aforesaid, that are not already actually possessed by or granted to any of our subjects, or possessed by the subjects of any other Christian Prince or State, with the fishing of all sorts of fish, whales, sturgeons and all other royal fishes, in the seas, bays, inlets, and rivers within the premises, and the fish therein taken, together with the royalty of the sea upon the coasts within the limits aforesaid, and all mines royal, as well discovered as not discovered, of gold, silver, gems and precious stones, to be found or discovered within the territories, limits and places aforesaid, and that the said land be from henceforth reckoned and reputed as one of our plantations or colonies in America, called "Rupert's Land."

And further we do, by these presents for us, our heirs and successors, make, create, and constitute the said Governor and Company for the time being, and their successors, the true and absolute lords and proprietors of the same territory, limits and places, and of all other the premises, saving always the faith, allegiance and sovereign dominion due to us, our heirs and successors, . . . yielding and paying yearly to us, our heirs and successors, for the same, two elks and two black beavers, whensoever and as often as we, our heirs and successors, shall happen to enter into the said countries, territories and regions hereby granted. . . .

It shall and may be lawful to and for the said Governor and Company, and their successors, . . . to make, ordain and constitute such and so many reasonable laws, constitutions, orders and ordinances as to them, or the greater part of them, being then and there present, shall seem necessary and convenient for the good government of the said Company, and of all governors of colonies, forts and plantations, factors, masters, mariners and other officers employed or to be employed in any of the territories and lands aforesaid, and in any of their voyages, and for the better advancement and continuance of the said trade or traffic and plantations, . . . The said Governor and Company, . . . shall and may lawfully impose, ordain, limit and provide such pains, penalties and punishments upon all offenders, contrary to such laws, constitutions, orders and ordinances, or any of them, as . . . shall seem necessary, requisite or convenient for the observation of the same laws, . . .

And moreover, our will and pleasure is, and by these presents, for us, our heirs and successors, we do give and grant unto the said Governor and Company, and their successors, free liberty and license, in case they conceive it necessary, to send either ships of war, men or ammunition into any of their plantations, forts, factories, or places of trade aforesaid, for the security and defence of the same, and to choose commanders and officers over them, and to give them power and authority, by commission under their common seal, or otherwise, to continue to make peace or war with any prince or people whatsoever, that are not Christians, in any place where the said Company shall have any plantations, forts or factories, or adjacent thereto, and shall be most for the advantage and benefit of the said Governor and Company and of their trade; . . .

We do grant unto the said Governor and Company, and to their successors, full power and lawful authority to seize upon the persons of all such English, or any other our subjects, which shall sail into Hudson's Bay, or in-

habit in any of the countries, islands or territories hereby
granted to the said Governor and Company, without their
leave and license, . . .

Witness ourselves at Winchester, the second day of
May, in the two and twentieth year of our reign.

By Writ of the Privy Seal.
PIGOTT

— 5 —

A DESCRIPTION OF A SHIP OF SIXTY TUNS, WHICH WE BUILT NEAR THE STREIGHTS OF THE LAKE ERIE, DURING THE WINTER AND SPRING OF THE YEAR 1679[5]

*The Griffon was the first ship to sail the upper lakes.
The following selections from the writings of Father
Louis Hennepin describe the building, launching, and loss
of the vessel. Hennepin is a controversial figure, and
much of his writing is discredited. But there does not
seem to be any reason to distrust these parts of his narrative. He was born in Belgium about the year 1640. While
young, he joined the Récollet order, a reformed offshoot
of the Franciscans. After serving in Canada from 1615
until 1629, the Récollets did not return to Canada until
1670. Hennepin himself came to America with La Salle
in 1675 and was chosen to accompany him in his ambi-*

[5] L. Hennepin, *A New Discovery of a Vast Country in America* (London, 1698), I, 48-52, 58-59, 62-63, 70-71.

*tious explorations. Hennepin was last reported as being in
a convent in Rome in 1701. Where and when he died are
unknown.*

✦   ✦   ✦

. . . On the 20th [of January, 1679] arrived M. de la
Salle from Fort Frontenac, from whence he was sent with
a great Barque to supply us with Provisions, Rigging,
and Tackling for the Ship we design'd to build at the
Mouth of the Lake Erie; but that Barque was unfortunately cast away on the Southern Coast of the Lake
Ontario, by the fault of two Pilots, who could not agree
about the Course they were to steer, tho' they were then
only within two Leagues of Niagara. The Sea-men have
call'd this Place the Mad-Cape. The Anchors and Cables
were sav'd, but several Canows made of Barks of Trees
with Goods and Commodities were lost. These disap-
pointments were such as would have disswaded from any
farther Enterprize all other Persons but such who had
form'd the generous Design of making a New Discovery
in the Country. . . .

On the 22th of the said Month, we went two Leagues
above the great Fall of Niagara, where we made a Dock
for Building the Ship we wanted for our Voyage. This
was the most convenient place we could pitch upon, being
upon a River which falls into the Streight between the
Lake Erie and the Great Fall of Niagara. The 26th, the
Keel of the Ship and some other Pieces being ready,
M. de la Salle sent the Master-Carpenter to desire me to
drive in the first Pin; but my Profession obliging me to
decline that Honour, he did it himself, and promis'd Ten
Louis d'Or's, to encourage the Carpenter and further the
Work. . . .

When I return'd to our Dock, I understood that most of
the Iroquese were gone to wage War with a Nation on
the other side of the Lake Erie. In the mean time, our
Men continu'd with great Application to build our Ship;
for the Iroquese who were left behind, being but a small
number, were not so insolent as before, though they came
now and then to our Dock, and express'd some Discon-
tent at what we were doing. One of them in particular,
feigning himself drunk, attempted to kill our Smith, but

was vigorously repuls'd by him with a red-hot Iron-barr, which, together with the Reprimand he receiv'd from me, oblig'd him to be gone. Some few Days after, a Savage Woman gave us notice, that the Tsonnontouans had resolv'd to burn our Ship in the Dock, and had certainly done it, had we not been always upon our Guard. . . .

The two Savages we had taken into our Service, went all this while a Hunting, and supply'd us with Wild-Goats, and other Beasts for our Subsistence; which encourag'd our Workmen to go on with their Work more briskly than before, insomuch that in a short time our Ship was in a readiness to be launch'd; which we did, after having bless'd the same according to the use of the Romish Church. We made all the haste we could to get it a-float, though not altogether finish'd, to prevent the Designs of the Natives, who had resolv'd to burn it.

The Ship was call'd the Griffin, alluding to the Arms of Count Frontenac, which have two Griffins for Supporters; and besides, M. la Salle us'd to say of this Ship, while yet upon the Stocks, That he would make the Griffin fly above the Ravens. We fir'd three Guns, and sung Te Deum, which was attended with loud Acclamations of Joy; of which those of the Iroquese, who were accidentally present at this Ceremony, were also Partakers; for we gave them some Brandy to drink, as well as to our Men, who immediately quitted their Cabins of Rinds of Trees, and hang'd their Hammocks under the Deck of the Ship, there to lie with more security than a-shoar. We did the like, insomuch that the very same Day we were all on board, and thereby out of the reach of the Insults of the Savages.

The Iroquese being return'd from Hunting Beavers, were mightily surpriz'd to see our Ship a-float, and call'd us Otkon, that is in their language, Most penetrating Wits: For they could not apprehend how in so short a time we had been able to build so great a Ship, though it was but 60 Tuns. It might have been indeed call'd a moving Fortress; for all the Savages inhabiting the Banks of Those Lakes and Rivers I have mention'd, for five hundred Leagues together, were fill'd with Fear as well as Admiration when they saw it. . . .

The Iroquese were then returning from a Warlike

Expedition with several Slaves, and were much surpriz'd
to see so big a Ship, which they compar'd to a Fort,
beyond their Limits. Several came on board, and seem'd
to admire above all things the bigness of our Anchors;
for they could not apprehend how we had been able to
bring them through the rapid Currents of the River St.
Laurence. This oblig'd them to use often the Word
Gannorom, which in their Language signifies, That is
wonderful. They wonder'd also to find there a Ship,
having seen none when they went; and did not know from
whence it came, it being about 250 Leagues from
Canada. . . .

On the 7th of August, 1679, we went on board, being in
all four and thirty Men, including two Recollects who
came to us, and sail'd from the Mouth of the Lake Erie,
steering our Course West-South-West, with a favourable
Wind; and though the Enemies of our Discovery had
given out, on purpose to deterr us from our Enterprize,
That the Lake Erie was full of Rocks and Sands, which
render'd the Navigation impracticable, we run about
twenty Leagues during the Night, though we sounded all
that while. The next Day the Wind being more favourable, we made above five and forty leagues, keeping at an
equal distance from the Banks of the Lake, and doubled
a Cape to the West-ward, which we call'd the Cape of
St. Francis. The next Day we doubled two other Capes,
and met with no manner of Rocks or Sands. We discover'd a pretty large Island towards the South-West,
about seven or eight Leagues from the Northern Coast;
that Island faces the Streight that comes from the Lake
Huron. . . .

On the 2d of September we weigh'd Anchor, and sail'd
into the Lake of the Illinois; and came to an Island just at
the Mouth of the Bay of the Puans, lying about forty
Leagues from Missilimakinak: . . . Our Ship was riding
in the Bay about thirty Paces from the furthermost Point
of Land, at a pretty good Anchorage, where we rode
safely, notwithstanding a violent Storm which lasted four
Days. . . .

M. la Salle, without asking any body's Advice, resolv'd
to send back his Ship to Niagara, laden with Furrs and
Skins to discharge his Debts; our Pilot and five Men

with him were therefore sent back, and order'd to return with all imaginable speed, to join us toward the Southern Parts of the Lake, where we should stay for them among the Illinois. They sailed the 18th of September with a Westerly Wind, and fir'd a Gun to take their leave. Tho' the Wind was favourable, it was never known what Course they steer'd, nor how they perish'd; for after all the Enquiries we have been able to make, we could never learn any thing else but the following Particulars.

The Ship came to an Anchor to the North of the Lake of the Illinois, where she was seen by some Savages, who told us that they advised our Men to sail along the Coast, and not towards the middle of the Lake, because of the Sands that make the Navigation dangerous when there is any high Wind. Our Pilot, as I said before, was dissatisfy'd, and would steer as he pleas'd, without hearkning to the Advice of the Savages, who, generally speaking, have more Sense than the Europeans think at first; but the Ship was hardly a League from the Coast, when it was toss'd up by a violent Storm in such a manner, that our Men were never heard of since; and it is suppos'd that the Ship struck upon a Sand, and was there bury'd. This was a great loss for M. la Salle and other Adventurers; for that Ship, with its Cargo, cost above sixty thousand Livres. . . .

— 6 —

THE FIRST ASSEMBLY IN CANADA, MAY 20, 1758[6]

Although England acquired Nova Scotia by the Treaty of Utrecht in April, 1713, she did little with the territory until the foundation of Halifax in 1749. The English purpose was to maintain Halifax and Nova Scotia itself as a military base to counter the French fortress of Louisbourg. But immigrants from England and New England, accustomed to self-government, demanded an assembly. While it is true that representative bodies had been known in the Thirteen Colonies since 1619, the granting of a General Assembly to Nova Scotia in 1758 was significant because it was the first representative body in what was destined to become the second British Empire and British Commonwealth. Five of the members in the first legislature had a New England background. The document printed here is the proclamation which set up the assembly.

✓   ✓   ✓

PROVINCE OF NOVA-SCOTIA
COUNCIL-CHAMBER, HALIFAX
20TH MAY, 1758

His Excellency the Governor, together with His Majesty's Council, having had under mature Consideration the necessary and most expedient Measures for carrying into Execution those Parts of His Majesty's Commission and Instructions which relate to the Calling General Assemblies within the Province, came to the following Resolutions thereon, *Viz.*

That a House of Representatives of the Inhabitants of

[6] From official printed copy.

this Province, be the Civil Legislature thereof, in Conjunction with His Majesty's Governor or Commander in Chief for the Time being, and His Majesty's Council of the said Province: The first House to be elected and convened in the following Manner, and to be stiled the GENERAL ASSEMBLY, *Viz.*

That there shall be elected for the Province at large, until the same shall be divided into Counties, Sixteen Members: For the Township of *Halifax,* Four: for the Township of *Lunenburg,* Two. . . .

That the House shall always consist of at least Eleven Members present, besides the Speaker, before they enter upon Business.

That no Person shall be chosen as a Member of the said House, or shall have a Right of voting in the Election of any Member of the said House, who shall be a Popish Recusant, or shall be under the Age of Twenty-one Years, or who shall not at the Time of such Election, be possessed in his own Right of a Freehold Estate within the District for which he shall be elected, or shall so vote, nor shall any Elector have more than one Vote for each Member to be chosen for the Province at large, or for any Township; and that each Freeholder present at such election, and giving his Vote for one Member for the Province at large, shall be obliged to vote also for the other Fifteen. . . .

CHA^{S.} LAWRENCE

By His Excellency's Command,
   with the Advice and Consent
   of His Majesty's Council
Jno. Duport, Sec: Conc:

— 7 —

ARTICLES OF CAPITULATION, QUEBEC, SEPTEMBER 18, 1759[7]

The battle of the Plains of Abraham is rightly considered one of the decisive battles in North America. Wolfe, the British commander, having spent the summer of 1759 off Quebec, was able to make a landing on September 13 and to engage Montcalm on the plain about a mile west of the city. The British were victorious though Wolfe was killed. Montcalm, the French commander, was fatally wounded. The remains of the French army withdrew to Montreal, leaving de Ramezay in command at Quebec to secure the best terms he could. He surrendered on September 18. Though not the last battle of the Seven Years, or French and Indian War, it marked the end. The surrender of Quebec foreshadowed the surrender of the whole country.

✓   ✓   ✓

Demanded by Mr. de Ramsay, the King's Lieutenant, commanding the high and low Towns of Quebec, Chief of the military order of St. Lewis, to His Excellency the General of the troops of His Britannic Majesty.— "The Capitulation demanded on the part of the enemy, "and granted by their Excellencies Admiral Saunders "and General Townshend, &c., &c., &c., is in manner "and form hereafter expressed." . . .

I

"The Garrison of the town, composed of Land forces, "marines and sailors, shall march out with their arms and

[7] Adam Shortt and Arthur G. Doughty, eds., *Documents relating to the Constitutional History of Canada, 1759-1791* (Ottawa, 1918), I, 5-7.

"baggage, drums beating, matches lighted, with two pieces
"of french cannon, and twelve rounds for each piece; and
"shall be embarked as conveniently as possible, to be sent
"to the first port in France." . . .

II

That the inhabitants shall be preserved in the possession of their houses, goods, effects, and privileges.—
"Granted, upon their laying down their arms."

III

That the inhabitants shall not be accountable for having
carried arms in the defence of the town, for as much as
they were compelled to it, and that the inhabitants of the
colonies, of both crowns, equally serve as militia.—
"Granted." . . .

VI

"The free exercise of the Roman religion is granted,
"likewise safeguards to all religious persons, as well as to
"the Bishop, who shall be at liberty to come and exercise,
"freely and with decency, the functions of his office,
"whenever he shall think proper, until the possession of
"Canada shall have been decided between their Britannic
"and most Christian Majesties." . . .

IX

That before delivering up the gate and the entrance of
the town to the English troops, their General will be
pleased to send some soldiers to be posted as safe-guards
upon the churches, convents, and principal habitations.—
"Granted." . . .

Duplicates hereof taken and executed by, and between
us, at the camp before Quebec, this 18th Day of September, 1759.

CHARLES SAUNDERS
GEORGE TOWNSHEND
DE RAMSAY

— 8 —

TREATY OF PARIS, FEBRUARY 10, 1763[8]

By the Treaty of Paris, France ceded Canada to Great Britain. All French territory on the mainland of North America, east of the Mississippi, now came under British control. The two small islands of St. Pierre and Miquelon off the south shore of Newfoundland were left to France as an unfortified shelter for French fishermen. The ceding of Canada brought to an end over a century and a half of French efforts at colonization.

✓   ✓   ✓

In the Name of the Most Holy and Undivided Trinity, Father, Son and Holy Ghost. So be it.

Be it known to all those whom it shall, or may, in any manner, belong, . . .

IV. His Most Christian Majesty renounces all pretensions which he has heretofore formed or might have formed to Nova Scotia or Acadia in all its parts, and guaranties the whole of it, and with all its dependencies, to the King of Great Britain: Moreover, his Most Christian Majesty cedes and guaranties to his said Britannick Majesty, in full right, Canada, with all its dependencies, as well as the island of Cape Breton, and all the other islands and coasts in the gulph and river of St. Lawrence, and in general, every thing that depends on the said countries, lands, islands, and coasts, with the sovereignty, property, possession, and all rights acquired by treaty, or otherwise, which the Most Christian King and the Crown of France have had till now over the said countries, lands,

[8] Shortt and Doughty, eds., *Documents relating to the Constitutional History of Canada, 1759-1791*, I, 113-116, 122.

islands, places, coasts, and their inhabitants, so that the Most Christian King cedes and makes over the whole to the said King, and to the Crown of Great Britain, and that in the most ample manner and form, without restriction, and without any liberty to depart from the said cession and guaranty under any pretence, or to disturb Great Britain in the possessions above mentioned. His Britannick Majesty, on his side, agrees to grant the liberty of the Catholick religion to the inhabitants of Canada: he will, in consequence, give the most precise and most effectual orders, that his new Roman Catholic subjects may profess the worship of their religion according to the rites of the Romish church, as far as the laws of Great Britain permit. His Britannick Majesty farther agrees, that the French inhabitants, or others who had been subjects of the Most Christian King in Canada, may retire with all safety and freedom wherever they shall think proper, and may sell their estates, provided it be to the subjects of his Britannick Majesty, and bring away their effects as well as their persons, without being restrained in their emigration, under any pretence whatsoever, except that of debts or of criminal prosecutions: The term limited for this emigration shall be fixed to the space of eighteen months, to be computed from the day of the exchange of the ratification of the present treaty. . . .

Done at Paris the tenth day of February, 1763.

BEDFORD, C.P.S.
(L.S.)
CHOISEUL, DUC DE PRASLIN
(L.S.)
EL MARQ. DE GRIMALDI
(L.S.)

— 9 —

THE ROYAL PROCLAMATION, OCTOBER 7, 1763[9]

Great Britain, having acquired the French territories in North America, was under the necessity of providing a system of government for the region. The Proclamation of 1763 provided four distinct governments: for East and West Florida, Grenada, and Quebec, the new name given to Canada.

In order to support the fur trade and preserve the hunting grounds of the Indians, the Proclamation limited the boundaries of Quebec and set up a vast reservation in the west. Settlers were excluded from this area, much to the chagrin of the residents of the Thirteen Colonies.

✓   ✓   ✓

WHEREAS We have taken into Our Royal Consideration the extensive and valuable Acquisitions in America, secured to our Crown by the late Definitive Treaty of Peace, concluded at Paris, the 10th Day of February last; . . . We have thought fit, . . . to erect, within the Countries and Islands ceded and confirmed to Us by the said Treaty, Four distinct and separate Governments, styled and called by the names of Quebec, East Florida, West Florida and Grenada, . . .

And whereas it will greatly contribute to the speedy settling our said new Governments, that our loving subjects should be informed of our Paternal care, for the security of the Liberties and Properties of those who are and shall become Inhabitants thereof, We have thought fit to publish and declare, . . . that so soon as the state

[9] Shortt and Doughty, eds., *Documents relating to the Constitutional History of Canada, 1759-1791*, I, 163-168.

and circumstances of the said Colonies will admit thereof, they shall, with the Advice and Consent of the Members of our Council, summon and call General Assemblies within the said Governments respectively, in such Manner and Form as is used and directed in those Colonies and Provinces in America which are under our immediate Government; . . .

And whereas it is just and reasonable, and essential to our interest, and the Security of our Colonies, that the several Nations or Tribes of Indians with whom We are connected, and who live under our Protection, should not be molested or disturbed in the Possession of such Parts of our Dominions and Territories as, not having been ceded to or purchased by Us, are reserved to them, or any of them, as their Hunting Grounds.—We do therefore, . . . declare it to be our Royal Will and Pleasure, that no Governor or Commander in Chief in any of our Colonies of Quebec, East Florida, or West Florida, do presume, upon any Pretence whatever, to grant Warrants of Survey, or pass any Patents for Lands beyond the Bounds of their respective Governments, as described in their Commissions; . . .

And, We do further declare it to be Our Royal Will and Pleasure, for the present as aforesaid, to reserve under our Sovereignty, Protection, and Dominion, for the use of the said Indians, all the Lands and Territories not included within the Limits of Our said Three new Governments, or within the Limits of the Territory granted to the Hudson's Bay Company, as also all the Lands and Territories lying to the Westward of the Sources of the Rivers which fall into the Sea from the West and North West as aforesaid; . . .

And we do, by the Advice of Our Privy Council, declare and enjoin, that the Trade with the said Indians shall be free and open to all our Subjects whatever, provided that every Person who may incline to Trade with the said Indians do take out a Licence for carrying on such Trade from the Governor or Commander in Chief of any of Our Colonies respectively where such Person shall reside, and also give Security to observe such Regulations as We shall at any Time think fit, by ourselves or by our Commissaries to be appointed for this Purpose, to direct and appoint for the Benefit of the said Trade: . . .

Given at our Court at St. James's the 7th Day of October 1763, in the Third Year of our Reign.

— 10 —

THE QUEBEC ACT, 1774[10]

The Proclamation of 1763 proved to be inadequate because the governor failed to set up the promised assembly. The Canadians feared for their land titles, and the provision of a bishop for the Church also created a problem. The Quebec Act of 1774 aimed to resolve the difficulties and also to ensure the loyalty of the French Canadians in any struggle which might arise in America. The Act specifically revoked the provision for an assembly; extended the boundaries of Quebec to the Ohio and Mississippi Rivers; continued English criminal but substituted French civil law in the province, thus guaranteeing the feudal system of land tenure; legalized the collection of tithes by the Roman Catholic Church and reaffirmed the freedom of the Canadians to worship as Roman Catholics. These provisions antagonized the American Colonies and added fuel to the fires of revolution. The Act is important as it is considered the foundation of French Canadian liberties in Canada today.

An Act for making more effectual Provision for the Government of the Province of *Quebec* in *North America*.

. . . And, for the more perfect Security and Ease of the Minds of the Inhabitants of the said Province, it is

[10] Shortt and Doughty, eds., *Documents relating to the Constitutional History of Canada, 1759-1791*, I, 570-574.

hereby declared, That His Majesty's Subjects, professing
the Religion of the Church of *Rome* of an in the said
province of *Quebec,* may have, hold, and enjoy, the free
Exercise of the Religion of the Church of *Rome,* subject
to the King's Supremacy, declared and established by an
Act, made in the First Year of the Reign of Queen *Elizabeth,* over all the Dominions and Countries which then
did, or thereafter should belong, to the Imperial Crown
of this Realm; and that the Clergy of the said Church
may hold, receive, and enjoy, their accustomed Dues and
Rights, with respect to such Persons only as shall profess
the said Religion.

Provided nevertheless, That it shall be lawful for His
Majesty, His Heirs or Successors, to make such Provi-
sion out of the rest of the said accustomed Dues and
Rights, for the Encouragement of the Protestant Religion
and for the Maintenance and Support of a Protestant
Clergy within the said Province, as he or they shall, from
Time to Time, think necessary and expedient. . . .

And be it further enacted by the Authority aforesaid,
That all His Majesty's *Canadian* Subjects, within the
Province of *Quebec,* the religious Orders and Communi-
ties only excepted, may also hold and enjoy their Prop-
erty and Possessions, together with all Customs and
Usages relative thereto, and all other their Civil Rights,
in as large, ample, and beneficial Manner, as if the said
Proclamation, Commissions, Ordinances, and other Acts
and Instruments, had not been made, and as may consist
with their Allegiance to His Majesty, and Subjection to the
Crown and Parliament of *Great Britain;* and that in all
Matters of Controversy, relative to Property and Civil
Rights, Resort shall be had to the Laws of *Canada,* as
the Rule for the Decision of the same; . . .

And whereas the Certainty and Lenity of the Criminal
Law of *England,* and the Benefits and Advantages result-
ing from the Use of it, have been sensibly felt by the
Inhabitants, from an Experience of more than Nine
Years, during which it has been uniformly administered;
be it therefore further enacted by the Authority aforesaid, That the same shall continue to be administered,
and shall be observed as Law in the Province of *Quebec,* . . .

— 11 —

COOK'S VOYAGE TO THE PACIFIC OCEAN. TRANSACTIONS AMONGST THE NATIVES OF NORTH AMERICA, MARCH AND APRIL 1778[11]

Captain James Cook was the first Englishman to see any part of the coast of British Columbia. Cook, one of the world's great circumnavigators, was born in November, 1728. After a varied career, including surveying the channels of the St. Lawrence and the coasts of Newfoundland and Labrador, in 1768 he was commissioned to command an expedition to the Pacific to observe the transit of Venus. His success in this expedition led to his appointment to explore the Pacific in 1772. In 1776 he began a third voyage to the North Pacific. Cook, in command of the Resolution, *was accompanied by Captain Charles Clerke, in command of the* Discovery. *The document printed here describes Cook's arrival at Nootka Sound and the natives he found there. The trade in sea-otter skins begun by Cook's expedition resulted in a rush to Nootka of ships of many nations. Cook himself was killed at Hawaii while on his voyage home, early in 1779.*

✓   ✓   ✓

. . . At length, at nine o'clock in the morning of the 29th [of March, 1778], as we were standing to the north-east, we again saw the land, which, at noon, extended from north-west by west, to east south-east. . . . The appearance of the country differed much from that of the

[11] *The Three Voyages of Captain James Cook Round the World* (London, 1821), VI, 243-251, 262-263.

parts which we had before seen, being full of high mountains, whose summits were covered with snow; but the
valleys between them, and the grounds on the sea coast,
high as well as low, were covered to a considerable
breadth with high straight trees, that formed a beautiful
prospect, as of one vast forest. . . .

As we drew nearer the coast, we perceived the appearance of two inlets; one in the north-west, and the other
in the north-east corner of the bay. As I could not fetch
the former, I bore up the latter. . . .

We no sooner drew near the inlet, than we found the
coast to be inhabited; and at the place where we were first
becalmed, three canoes came off to the ship. In one of
these were two men, in another six, and in the third ten.
Having come pretty near us, a person in one of the two
last stood up, and made a long harangue, inviting us to
land, as we guessed by his gestures. At the same time, he
kept strewing handfuls of feathers towards us; and some
of his companions threw handfuls of red dust or powder
in the same manner. The person who played the orator,
wore the skin of some animal, and held in each hand
something which rattled as he kept shaking it. After tiring
himself with his repeated exhortations, of which we did
not understand a word, he was quiet; and then others
took it, by turns, to say something, though they acted
their part neither so long, nor with so much vehemence
as the other. We observed that two or three had their
hair quite strewed over with small white feathers, and
others had large ones stuck into different parts of the
head. After the tumultuous noise had ceased, they lay at
a little distance from the ship, and conversed with each
other in a very easy manner, nor did they seem to show
the least surprise or distrust. Some of them, now and
then got up, and said something after the manner of their
first harangues; and one sung a very agreeable air, with
a degree of softness and melody which we could not have
expected; the word *haela,* being often repeated as the
burden of the song. The breeze which soon after sprung
up, bringing us nearer to the shore, the canoes began to
come off in greater numbers; and we had, at one time,
thirty-two of them near the ship, carrying from three to
seven or eight persons each, both men and women. Sev-

eral of these stood up in their canoes haranguing, and making gestures after the manner of our first visitors. One canoe was remarkable for a singular head, which had a bird's eye and bill, of an enormous size, painted on it; and a person who was in it, who seemed to be a chief, was no less remarkable for his uncommon appearance; having many feathers hanging from his head, and being painted in an extraordinary manner. He held in his hand a carved bird of wood, as large as a pigeon, with which he rattled as the person first-mentioned had done; and was no less vociferous in his harangue, which was attended with some expressive gestures.

Though our visitors behaved very peaceably, and could not be suspected of any hostile intention, we could not prevail upon any of them to come on board. They showed great readiness, however, to part with any thing they had, and took from us whatever we offered them in exchange; but were more desirous of iron, than of any other of our articles of commerce; appearing to be perfectly acquainted with the use of that metal. Many of the canoes followed us to our anchoring-place; and a group of about ten or a dozen of them remained along-side the Resolution most part of the night.

These circumstances gave us a reasonable ground of hope, that we should find this a comfortable station to supply all our wants, and to make us forget the hardships and delays experienced during a constant succession of adverse winds, and boisterous weather, almost ever since our arrival upon the coast of America. . . .

The ships having happily found so excellent shelter in an inlet, the coasts of which appeared to be inhabited by a race of people, whose inoffensive behaviour promised a friendly intercourse, the next morning, after coming to anchor, I lost no time in endeavouring to find a commodious harbour, where we might station ourselves during our continuance in the sound. . . .

A great many canoes, filled with natives, were about the ships all day; and a trade commenced betwixt us and them, which was carried on with the strictest honesty on both sides. The articles which they offered to sale were skins of various animals, such as bears, wolves, foxes, deer, racoons, polecats, martins; and, in particular, of the

sea otters, which are found at the islands east of Kam-
tschatka. Besides the skins in their native shape, they also
brought garments made of them, and another sort of
clothing made of the bark of a tree, or some plant like
hemp; weapons, such as bows, arrows, and spears; fish-
hooks, and instruments of various kinds; wooden vizors of
many different monstrous figures; a sort of woollen stuff,
or blanketing; bags filled with red ochre; pieces of carved
work; beads; and several other little ornaments of thin
brass and iron, shaped like a horse-shoe, which they hang
at their noses; and several chissels, or pieces of iron fixed
to handles. From their possessing which metals, we could
infer that they had either been visited before by some
civilized nation, or had connections with tribes on their
continent, who had communication with them. But the
most extraordinary of all the articles which they brought
to the ships for sale were human skulls, and hands not yet
quite stripped of the flesh, which they made our people
plainly understand they had eaten; and, indeed some of
them had evident marks that they had been upon the fire.
. . . For the various articles which they brought, they
took in exchange knives, chissels, pieces of iron and tin,
nails, looking-glasses, buttons, or any kind of metal. Glass
beads they were not fond of; and cloth of every sort they
rejected. . . .

The fame of our arrival brought a great concourse of
the natives to our ships in the course of this day. We
counted above a hundred canoes at one time, which might
be supposed to contain, at an average, five persons each.
. . . A considerable number of natives visited us
daily. . . .

Every thing being now ready in the morning of the 26th
[of April, 1778], I intended to put to sea, but both wind
and tide being against us, was obliged to wait till
noon. . . .

— 12 —

A LOYALIST LETTER, APRIL 26, 1784 [12]

*With the coming of peace in 1783, after the American
Revolution, the Loyalists or Tories (the name depended
on who was using it) realized that any hope of happily
remaining in the new republic was gone. In addition to
those who moved to England and the West Indies, perhaps thirty thousand (higher figures are given) migrated
to Nova Scotia and about six (some claim ten) thousand
migrated to Quebec. Prince Edward Island also received
a share. The two major movements resulted in the setting
up of two new provinces, New Brunswick, separated from
Nova Scotia in 1784; and Upper Canada (later called
Ontario), separated from Quebec in 1791. The immigration of the Loyalists for many years colored Canadian history in a way out of all proportion to their numbers. The
document given here tells something of the hardships and
hopes of the displaced persons of 1784. It is a letter written from Halifax by Colonel Edward Winslow, a direct
descendant of Edward Winslow of Plymouth Colony, to
Ward Chipman.*

                    ✓   ✓   ✓

. . . I have seen, my dear Chipman (in the country
which I have formerly described to you), a vast collection
of valuable men of different orders,—men, respectable
for their conduct, with their families and the little remains
of their property—unattended to, and ungoverned. I saw
all those Provincial Regiments (which we have so frequently mustered) landing in this inhospitable climate, in

[12] W. O. Raymond, ed., *Winslow Papers, A.D. 1776-1826*
    (Saint John, N.B., 1901), 188-193.

the month of October, without shelter and without knowing where to find a place to reside. The chagrine of the
officers was not to me so truly affecting as the poignant
grief of the men. Those respectable Serjeants of Robinson's, Ludlow's, Cruger's, Fanning's, &c., corps (once
hospitable yeomen of the country) were addressing me in
a language which almost murdered me as I heard it. . . .
It stimulated me to propose to General Fox (who was
also witness to their distress) the plan of forming a
separate Government, as the only possible means of effectual relief . . . It must be for the interest as well as the
honor of the British Government, to save from despair so
many of its faithful subjects. . . .

To form a judgment of the quantity of Lumber which
the country produces, consider what has been the last
year's consumption in this province. The towns of Shelburne, Digby, and those on St. John's River, and many
inferior towns have been built in the course of last Year
and they now contain many thousand houses. The materials for building those houses have been supplied without
any great assistance from the New Settlers, and the im-
portation from the States has been very inconsiderable,
because in most of those places the New Settlers have
(injudiciously) refused to traffic with them. It is fair
reasoning to say—If such considerable quantities of Lumber could be supplied (on an emergency) by the former
inhabitants (who God knows are not remarkable for their
industry) Surely it will increase immensely when a
multitude of spirited men shall find it an object worth
their attention. The fund of timber is literally inexhaustible. . . .

Omnipotence cannot effect the creation of more perfect
streams for mills than are to be found in all these places,
and the transportation of lumber from the places of sawing to the places of Export is rendered perfectly easy
because the currents always sett towards the latter. There
was nothing wanting but labourers, to procure almost any
quantity of lumber. The late acquisition of inhabitants—
obviates that difficulty. The kind of lumber which is used
for building, and which is most essential, such as Frames,
Joists, Plank, Boards, Clap-boards, & Shingles will be
exported in great abundance from hence—immediately.

And so will Hoops, the Birch-hoops it is agreed are as durable and valuable as any in the World. . . .

I shall say but little on the subject of Fish because it must occur to every man of common sense, that if the New-England Traders could find a profit in sending their vessels to this coast for Fish,—those who inhabit its borders can carry on the business to much greater advantage. The exertions now making are very spirited and I have no doubt that the exports of Fish from Shelburne & the other new places added to the former usual exports from the old ports will be an ample supply for the West Indies this year.

Horses are reared with more facility in Canada & about St. John's than in any country I ever saw, and they are the best Hacks in the world.

Beef & Pork is produced in great abundance on the peninsula of Nova-Scotia, more than is necessary for the inhabitants. Witness the quantities that were brought to us during the siege of Boston.

I cannot speak or write of that country about the river St. John's without making use of such extravagant expressions as have a tendency to lessen the weight of my testimonies in its favor. I acknowledge myself to be a little romantic, but I will appeal to General Fox & others who have observed it without being so much in raptures, whether they ever beheld a more delightful grass country, better cattle, or better grain, or more abundant crops. . . .

Lord Sydney's declaration quoted in your letter, "That he will make Nova-Scotia the envy of the American States," has excited a kind of general gratitude; I cannot describe it. Other ministers and Great men have, by their patronage of new settlers, relieved individuals from distress, and rendered services to their country, but it is a Godlike task that Lord Sydney has undertaken. Such an event as the present, never happened before—perhaps never will happen again. There are assembled here an immense multitude (not of dissolute vagrants such as commonly make the first efforts to settle new countries,) but gentlemen of education—Farmers, formerly independent—& reputable mechanics, who by the fortune of war have been deprived of their property. They are as firmly attached to the British constitution as if they never had made a sacrifice. Here they stand with their wives and their children looking up for protection, and requesting such regulations as are necessary to the weal of society. To save these from distress, to soothe and comfort them by extending indulgencies which at the same time are essentially beneficial to the country at large, is truly a noble duty. By Heaven we will be the envy of the American States. . . .

— 13 —

THE SEIGNIORIAL SYSTEM, OCTOBER 5, 1790[13]

First authorized in a charter to the Marquis de la Roche in 1598, seigniorial tenure continued in French Canada until 1854. During the more than two hundred and fifty years in which the system existed, it inevitably underwent evolution. The document below describes the system as it developed by 1790, as reported by the Solicitor-General of Quebec. His account is in the form of answers to questions put to him by members of the Council of Quebec.

✓　　　　✓　　　　✓

. . . *Question* 1.—"Upon what tenures were the lands of this country granted by the French Crown?"

The civil constitution of Canada was established upon the feudal system; large tracts of land were granted by the French Crown *en fief et seigneurie;* these estates are

[13] W. B. Munro, ed., *Documents Relating to the Seigniorial Tenure in Canada 1598-1854* (Toronto, The Champlain Society, 1908), 250-256.

styled *biens nobles;* small parcels and town lots were granted by an ignoble tenure, called *roture.*

There are some, a very few, allodial grants; the tenure is termed *franc aleu noble* and *franc aleu roturier;* a fewer still by that tenure which is of a spiritual nature called *pure aumône,* or frankalmoign.

Question 2.—"What kind of tenure was most prevalent and what may be stated in probable conjecture for the proportion between them?"

In the country, the tenure *en fief et seigneurie* was almost universal. In the town of Quebec, several small parcels were granted upon the same tenure; and there, as well as at Three Rivers and adjoining to the forts of Crown Point, Detroit, &c., small parcels or lots were granted *en roture.*

The proportion in favour of fiefs and seigneuries (alluding to the royal grants) is beyond comparison greater than all the other tenures. . . .

Question 4.—"What were the legal burdens upon the grantee of the Crown in reservations, conditions, rents, and services; or what were the benefits accruing to the French Crown from the nature of the grant, founded in the usual reservations, or by the general laws of the Country?"

The grantee and his heirs and assigns, by the tenor of this grant and by the law of the country were bound to render fealty and homage to the King (by his representative) at the Castle of St. Lewis in this city; the vassal was bound at the same time, or within forty days after to deliver to the King's representative an *aveu et denombrement,* that is to say, a particular statement of his title, the extent of his fief, its dependencies, appurtenances, and prerogatives whether he had a right to hold courts of justice, high, inferior, or low justice, any and which of them; the amount of the rent of the clerk's and notary's offices, fines, and other rights; his manor-house, the lands of his domain, the quantity and quality of his arable, meadow, pasture, and wood lands, what ponds and lakes, what farmhouses and other buildings he had on his domain, the boundaries of the farms, their revenue and to whom let, or whether he cultivated them himself, the annual amount of the *cens,* rents, and other dues, with the number and names of his *censitaires* or *terre-tenants,* or others subject to pay rent to him; the rights and services he owed on account of his fief, whether he had right of mill; the lands granted *en roture* on his estate; and a particular designation of the *arriere* or rear fiefs; how he became entitled to his fief and seigneurie, whether by succession (and particularly whether in the line direct or collateral), by purchase, gift, or how otherwise.

Upon the sale or other mutation of the fief (except in the direct line) the fine called *droit de quint,* or a fifth part of the amount of the purchase money was payable to the King, at the time of rendering fealty and homage, in respect of lands governed by the Custom of Paris, which is the general law of the country; . . .

These are legal burdens.

A few old grants made by the India Company stipulated that on every mutation a medal of half an ounce or an ounce of gold (*une maille d'or*) should be paid the Company in lieu of the *quint.*

The usual reservations and conditions in the more ancient grants were:

1. That the grantee should, within a year and a day, build an habitation upon, and actually inhabit the lands (*tenir feu et lieu*) and cultivate and improve the same (*déserter et mettre en valeur*) and cause his ter-tenants (*censitaires*) to do the same within the same period; (some grants mention that the lands are to be stocked with cattle in two years;) in default of which the King should of right re-enter into the possession of the lands granted; but a formal process for the reunion was, however, thought necessary, and always prosecuted by the attorney-general.

2. That the grantee should preserve all oak trees growing on his domain, and cause all oak trees fit for the construction of the King's ships to be preserved by his sub-feudatories (*censitaires*).

3. That the grantee should give immediate advice to the King or his governor and intendant, of the discovery of all mines, ores, and minerals (*mines, minières, et minéraux*) found in the lands granted; with exception only to two grants, wherein they are expressly given to the grantees.

4. That the grantee should get the grant ratified by the King, generally within the period of one year.

5. That the grantees should permit the necessary roads to be laid out for public utility, and cause a clause to be inserted in their concessions to the ter-tenants that they should do the same.

The more modern grants contain the same reservations and conditions, but they also contain additional stipulations namely;

6. That in case the King should have occasion for any part of the land granted for the purpose of building forts, batteries, places of arms, stores, or other public works, he should be at liberty to take the same, together with the trees and timber that should be necessary, and also firewood for the supply of the garrisons, within the extent of the lands granted, without being held or bound to make any compensation to the grantee.

7. That the grantee should allow the free use of the beaches to all fishermen, except such part as he might stand in need of for his own fisheries.

8. That the grantee should concede lands to his sub-feudatories at the accustomed rents and dues (*cens et rentes et redevances accoutumés*) for every acre in front by forty in depth, about a fourth part only of the grants contain this clause.

9. In many of the latest grants the King reserves the right of taking oak timber, masts, and yards (*mâtures*), and all other timber proper for the construction and equipment of his ships, without making any compensation for the same; and in one grant the King reserves the red or pitch pine for making tar. . . .

— 14 —

THE CONSTITUTIONAL ACT, 1791 [14]

*The immigration of United Empire Loyalists into the
western parts of British North America during and
after the American Revolution introduced into the country a new English-speaking element, accustomed to representative institutions and freehold land tenure. The Quebec Act of 1774, providing as it did French civil law and
no assembly, was entirely inadequate for these new settlers. The western Loyalists quickly expressed their demands, not failing to point out that the Loyalists in Nova
Scotia enjoyed privileges which they lacked. In 1791 the
British Parliament passed the Canada Act, now usually
called the Constitutional Act, which provided for the division of Quebec into Lower and Upper Canada (subsequently effected by proclamation) and set up assemblies
in both parts, and freehold land tenure in Upper Canada.*

An Act to repeal certain Parts of an Act, passed in the
Fourteenth Year of His Majesty's Reign, intituled, *An
Act for making more effectual Provision for the Government of the Province of* Quebec, *in* North America; and
to make further Provision for the Government of the
said Province.

Whereas an Act was passed in the Fourteenth Year of
the Reign of His present Majesty, intituled, *An Act for
making more effectual Provision for the Government of
the Province of* Quebec *in* North America: And whereas
the said Act is in many Respects inapplicable to the present Condition and Circumstances of the said Province:

[14] Shortt and Doughty, eds., *Documents relating to the Consti-
     tutional History of Canada, 1759-1791,* II, 1031-1032,
     1035-1036, 1038, 1041, 1043-1045, 1048.

And whereas it is expedient and necessary that further Provision should now be made for the good Government and Prosperity thereof; May it therefore please Your most Excellent Majesty that it may be enacted . . . That so much of the said Act as in any Manner relates to the Appointment of a Council for the Affairs of the said Province of *Quebec* . . . the same is hereby repealed.

II. And whereas His Majesty has been pleased to signify, by His Message to both Houses of Parliament, His Royal Intention to divide His Province of *Quebec* into Two separate Provinces, to be called *The Province of Upper Canada,* and *The Province of Lower Canada;* be it enacted by the Authority aforesaid, That there shall be within each of the said Provinces respectively a Legislative Council, and an Assembly, to be severally composed and constituted in the Manner herein-after described; . . . and that all such Laws, being passed by the Legislative Council and Assembly of either of the said Provinces respectively, and assented to by His Majesty, His Heirs or Successors, . . . shall be, and the same are hereby declared to be, . . . valid and binding to all Intents and Purposes whatever, within the Province in which the same shall have been so passed.

III. And be it further enacted by the Authority aforesaid, that for the Purpose of constituting such Legislative Council as aforesaid in each of the said Provinces respectively, it shall and may be lawful for His Majesty . . . to authorize and direct the Governor or Lieutenant Governor . . . to summon to the said Legislative Council, to be established in each of the said Provinces respectively, a sufficient Number of discreet and proper Persons, being not fewer than Seven to the Legislative Council for the Province of *Upper Canada,* and not fewer than Fifteen to the Legislative Council for the Province of *Lower Canada;* . . .

XIII. And be it further enacted by the Authority aforesaid, That, for the Purpose of constituting such Assembly as aforesaid, in each of the said Provinces respectively, it shall and may be lawful for His Majesty, His Heirs or Successors, by an Instrument under His or their Sign Manual, to authorize and direct the Governor or Lieutenant Governor, or Person administering the Government in each of the said Provinces respectively, within the Time herein-after mentioned, and thereafter from Time to Time, as Occasion shall require, in His Majesty's Name, and by an Instrument under the Great Seal of such Province, to summon and call together an Assembly in and for such Province. . . .

XX. And be it further enacted by the Authority aforesaid, That the Members for the several Districts, or Counties, or Circles of the said Provinces respectively, shall be chosen by the Majority of Votes of such Persons as shall severally be possessed, for their own use and Benefit, of Lands or Tenements within such District, or County, or Circle, as the Case shall be, such Lands being by them held in Freehold, or in Fief, or in Roture, or by Certificate derived under the Authority of the Governor and Council of the Province of *Quebec*, and being of the yearly Value of Forty Shillings Sterling, or upwards, over and above all Rents and Charges payable out of or in respect of the same; and that the Members for the several Towns or Townships within the said Provinces respectively shall be chosen by the Majority of Votes of such Persons as either shall severally be possessed, for their own Use and Benefit, of a Dwelling House and Lot of Ground in such Town or Township, such Dwelling House and Lot of Ground being by them held in like Manner as aforesaid, and being of the yearly Value of Five Pounds Sterling, or upwards, or, as having been resident within the said Town or Township for the Space of Twelve Calendar Months next before the Date of the Writ of Summons for the Election, shall *bona fide* have paid One Year's Rent for the Dwelling House in which they shall have so resided, at the Rate of Ten Pounds Sterling *per Annum,* or upwards. . . .

XXX. And be it further enacted by the Authority aforesaid, That whenever any Bill which has been passed by the Legislative Council, and by the House of Assembly, in either of the said Provinces respectively, shall be presented, for His Majesty's Assent, to the Governor or Lieutenant Governor of such Province, or to the Person administering His Majesty's Government therein, . . . he is hereby authorized and required to declare, . . . that he assents to such Bill in His Majesty's Name, or that he withholds His Majesty's Assent from such Bill, or that he reserves such Bill for the Signification of His Majesty's Pleasure thereon.

XXXI. Provided always, and be it further enacted by the Authority aforesaid, That whenever any Bill, which shall have been so presented for His Majesty's Assent to such Governor, Lieutenant Governor, or Person administering the Government, . . . he is hereby required, by the first convenient Opportunity, to transmit to One of His Majesty's principal Secretaries of State an authentick Copy of such Bill so assented to ; and that it shall and may be lawful, at any Time within Two Years after such Bill shall have been so received by such Secretary of State, for His Majesty, His Heirs or Successors, by His or their Order in Council, to declare His or their Disallowance of such Bill, . . .

XXXV. And whereas, by the above-mentioned Act, passed in the Fourteenth Year of the Reign of His present Majesty, it was declared, That the Clergy of the Church of *Rome,* in the Province of *Quebec,* might hold, receive, and enjoy their accustomed Dues and Rights, with respect to such Persons only as should profess the said Religion; provided nevertheless, that it should be lawful for His Majesty, His Heirs or Successors, to make such Provision out of the rest of the said accustomed Dues and Rights, for the Encouragement of the Protestant Religion, and for the Maintenance and Support of a Protestant Clergy within the said Province, as he or they should from Time to Time think necessary and expedient: . . . be it enacted by the Authority aforesaid, That the said Declaration and Provision contained in the said above-mentioned Act, and also the said Provision so made by His Majesty in consequence thereof, by His Instructions above recited, shall remain and continue to be of full Force and Effect in each of the said Two Provinces of *Upper Canada* and *Lower Canada* respectively, except in so far as the said Declaration or Provisions respectively, or any Part thereof, shall be expressly varied or repealed by any Act or Acts which may be passed by the Legislative Council and Assembly of the said Provinces respectively, and assented to by His Majesty, His Heirs or Successors, under the Restriction herein-after provided.

XXXVI. . . . be it enacted by the Authority aforesaid, That it shall and may be lawful for His Majesty, His Heirs or Successors, to authorize the Governor or Lieutenant Governor of each of the said Provinces respectively, or the Person administering the Government therein, to make, from and out of the Lands of the Crown within such Provinces, such Allotment and Appropriation of Lands, for the Support and Maintenance of a Protestant Clergy . . . and that such Lands, so allotted and appropriated, shall be, as nearly as the Circumstances and Nature of the Case will admit, of the like Quality as the Lands in respect of which the same are so allotted and appropriated, and shall be, as nearly as the same can be estimated at the Time of making such Grant, equal in Value to the Seventh Part of the Lands so granted. . . .

XXXVIII. And be it further enacted by the Authority aforesaid, That it shall and may be lawful for His Majesty, His Heirs or Successors, to authorize the Governor or Lieutenant Governor of each of the said Provinces respectively, . . . to constitute and erect, within every Township or Parish which now is or hereafter may be formed, constituted, or erected within such Province, One or more Parsonage or Rectory, or Parsonages or Rectories, according to the Establishment of the Church of *England;* and from Time to Time, by an Instrument under the Great Seal of such Province, to endow every such Parsonage or Rectory with so much or such Part of the Lands so allotted and appropriated as aforesaid, . . .

XLIII. And be it further enacted by the Authority aforesaid, That all Lands which shall be hereafter granted within the said Province of *Upper Canada* shall be granted in Free and Common Soccage, . . . and that in every Case where Lands shall be hereafter granted within the said Province of *Lower Canada,* and where the Grantee thereof shall desire the same to be granted in Free and Common Soccage, the same shall be so granted; . . .

— 15 —

PROCLAMATIONS CONCERNING UNITED EMPIRE LOYALISTS, APRIL 6, 1796 AND DECEMBER 15, 1798 [15]

*Many, perhaps a third, of the American colonists re-
mained loyal to Great Britain during the American Revolution. Since many lost all their possessions and were
driven from their homes in the Thirteen Colonies, the
British Crown was obligated to do something for them.
At first the problem was simply one of relief, but the
long term solution called for some permanent provision.
Since most Loyalists had lost land, they were reimbursed
with land. The following proclamations describe the steps
taken to recognize the sacrifices of the Loyalists in Upper Canada (Ontario). At the same time they provide a
definition of what constituted a United Empire Loyalist.
He must have joined the Royal Standard before the
treaty of 1783 and have been resident in Upper Canada
before July 28, 1798.*

✔   ✔   ✔

PROCLAMATION
[6th April, 1796]

By His Excellency John G. Simcoe, Esq., Lieutenant
Governor and Major General of His Majesty's Forces,
&c. &c. &c. in Upper Canada.

Whereas it appears by the minutes of the Council of
the late Province of Quebec, dated Monday the ninth day

---

[15] Alexander Fraser, *Fourth Report of the Bureau of Archives
for the Province of Ontario, 1906* (Toronto, 1907), 184-
185, 196-197.

of November 1789, to have been the desire of his Excellency Lord Dorchester the Governor-General "To put a *mark of honor* upon the families who had adhered to the Unity of the Empire, and joined the Royal Standard in America, before the treaty of separation in the year 1783," and for that purpose it was then "Ordered by his Excellency in Council, that the several Land Boards (should) take course in preserving a registry of the names of all persons falling under the description aforementioned, to the end that their posterity might be discriminated from (the then) future settlers in the parish registers and rolls of the militia of their respective districts, and other public remembrances of the Province, as proper objects, by their persevering in the fidelity and conduct so honourable to their ancestors, for distinguished benefits and privileges;" but as such registry has not been generally made; and as it is still necessary to ascertain the persons and families, who may have distinguished themselves as abovementioned; as well for the causes set forth, as for the purposes of fulfilling his Majesty's gracious intention of settling such persons and families upon the lands now about to be confirmed to them, without the incidental expences attending such grants:— Now KNOW YE, that I have thought proper, by and with the advice and consent of the executive council, to direct, and do hereby direct all persons, claiming to be confirmed by deed under the seal of the province in their several possessions, who adhered to the unity of the empire and joined the royal standard in America, before the treaty of separation in the year 1783, to ascertain the same upon oath before the magistrates in the michaelmas quarter-sessions assembled, now next ensuing the date of this proclamation, in such manner and form, as the magistrates are directed to receive the same;—and all persons will take notice that if they neglect to ascertain according to the mode above set forth, their claims to receive deeds without fee, they will not be considered as entitled, in this respect, to the benefit of having adhered to the unity of the empire and joined the royal standard in America before the treaty of separation in the year 1783.

Given under my hand and seal at arms, at the government house at York, this sixth day of April, in the year

of our Lord, one thousand seven hundred and ninety-six,
and in the thirty-sixth year of his Majesty's reign.

JOHN GRAVES SIMCOE

GOD SAVE THE KING!

By his Excellency's Command,

E. B. LITTLEHALES

PROCLAMATION
[15 Dec., 1798]

Peter Russell, Esq.; President, administering the Government of Upper Canada.

Whereas by Letters received from his Grace the Duke
of Portland, one of his Majesty's principal Secretaries of
State, since the issuing the Proclamation of the thirty-
first of October last, it appears, that in consequence of a
Representation made by the Executive Government of this
Province to his Majesty's Ministers, on the exemption of
the U. E. LOYALISTS and their CHILDREN from
every expense attending the Grants of Land made, or to
be made to them; his Majesty has been graciously pleased
to signify his Royal Pleasure that the FIRST LOYAL-
ISTS, and their SONS and DAUGHTERS, shall continue to receive his Majesty's BOUNTY of TWO HUN-
DRED ACRES each, as heretofore, free from any Expense whatever. And that it is to be understood, that this
Mark of the Royal Munificence is expressly confined to
those LOYALISTS only, who were actually resident in
the Province on or before the TWENTY-EIGHTH of
July last. . . .

Given under my Hand and Seal at Arms, in Council
at York, this fifteenth day of December, in the thirty-
ninth year of his Majesty's reign, and in the year of our
Lord one thousand seven hundred and ninety-eight.

PETER RUSSELL

By Command of the President in Council,

JOHN SMALL, C. E. C.

— 16 —

THE SURRENDER OF DETROIT, AUGUST 16, 1812[16]

The most unhappy episode in the history of Canadian-American relations was the War of 1812-15. Since the treaty of peace at its conclusion left the combatants as they had been, there was scarcely a victor. Out of the war, however, did develop the beginnings of a Canadian national feeling.

In their plans for invading Canada, the Americans, instead of concentrating their forces against Montreal, chose to attack the frontier of the lightly held Upper Canada. The defenders were commanded by Major-General Sir Isaac Brock, who used his few British regulars and Indians with great skill during the first months of the war, until his death at Queenston on October 13, 1812. One of the most brilliant incidents in the war was the capture of Detroit on August 16, 1812, by General Brock with forces vastly inferior in number to its American defenders. The victory had the double effect of halting the United States 1812 campaign and raising the morale of the wavering inhabitants and militiamen of Upper Canada. Brock's report to Sir George Prevost, Governor-General and Commander-in-Chief, and the terms of surrender, are given below.

✓   ✓   ✓

Hd Quarters Detroit
August 16th 1812

Sir,

I hasten to apprize Your Excellency of the Capture of

[16] William Wood, ed., *Select Documents of the Canadian War of 1812* (Toronto, The Champlain Society, 1920), I, 463, 470-471.

this very important Post—2500 troops have this day surrendered Prisoners of war, and about 25 pieces of Ordnance have been taken, without the sacrifice of a drop of British blood.

I had not more than 700 troops including Militia and about 600 Indians to accomplish this service—When I detail my good fortune Your Excellency will be astonished—I have been admirably supported by Colonel Procter, the whole of my staff and I may justly say every individual under my Command.

> Believe me
> Your's Excy faithful obedient
> Humble Servant
> ISAAC BROCK, M. G.

Camp at Detroit 16th Augt. 1812

Capitulation for the Surrender of Fort Detroit, entered into between Major Genl. Brock, commanding His Brittanick Majesty's Forces on the one part and Brigr. General Hull Commanding the North Western Army of the United States on the other part.

1st. Fort Detroit with all the Troops, Regulars as well as Militia, will be immediately surrendered to the British forces under the Command of Major Genl. Brock, and will be considered Prisoners of War, with the exception of such of the Militia of the Michigan territory who have not joined the Army.

2nd. All public Stores, Arms and all public documents encluding every thing else of a public Nature, will be immediately given up.

3rd. Private Persons & Property of every description will be respected.

4th. His Excellency Brigr Genl Hull having expressed a desire, that a detachment from the State of Ohio on its way to join his Army, as well as one sent from Fort Detroit under the Command of Colonel McArthur should be included in this Capitulation, it is accordingly agreed to. It is however to be understood, that such part of the Ohio Militia as have not joined the Army, will be permitted to return to their homes, on condition that they will not serve during the War. Their arms will be delivered up, if belonging to the public.

5th. The Garrison will march out at the hour of twelve o'clock this day, & the British forces will take immediate possession of the fort.

(signed) J. MACDONELL Lt. Col Militia P.A.D.C.
          J. B. GLEGG Major A.D.C.
          JAMES MILLER Lt. Colonel 5th U.S. Infantry
          E. BRUSH Col. Commandg. 1st Regt. Michigan Militia

          Approved
(Signed)—W. HULL, B.-Genl. Comdg. N. W. Army
          Approved
(Signed)—ISAAC BROCK Major Genl.

— 17 —

THE RUSH-BAGOT AGREEMENT, 1817[17]

The Rush-Bagot Agreement, sometimes erroneously called a treaty, which it was not, is frequently cited as a symbol of the many years of peace which have marked Canadian-United States relations. The actual name of the document is "An Agreement Effected by Notes Concerning Naval Force on the Great Lakes." Since Sir Charles Bagot, the British Minister in Washington, and Richard Rush, the acting Secretary of State, drew up the agree-

[17] William M. Malloy, comp., *Treaties, Conventions, International Acts, Protocols and Agreements between the United States of America and Other Powers 1776-1909* (Washington, 1910), I, 628-630.

ment their names have come to be applied to it. The agreement was signed, not from any high moral principles but, almost certainly, for reasons of economy on both sides. The subsequent relations of the two nations show that the agreement was sound. As there has been much loose writing and thinking about the agreement, the full text of the British proposal, repeated verbatim in the presidential proclamation, is given here. The agreement was signed at Washington, April 28-29, 1817; ratification advised by the Senate, April 16, 1818; and proclaimed by the President, April 28, 1818. The binding nature of the agreement and its permanence are revealed by an exchange of notes between Canada and the United States in 1940 and 1942. The final statement of Canadian agreement is given.

✓   ✓   ✓

Washington, April 28, 1817

The Undersigned, His Britannick Majesty's Envoy Extraordinary and Minister Plenipotentiary, has the honour to acquaint Mr. Rush, that having laid before His Majesty's Government the correspondence which passed last year between the Secretary of the Department of State and the Undersigned upon the subject of a proposal to reduce the Naval Force of the respective Countries upon the American Lakes, he has received the commands of His Royal Highness The Prince Regent to acquaint the Government of the United States, that His Royal Highness is willing to accede to the proposition made to the Undersigned by the Secretary of the Department of State in his note of the 2d of August last.

His Royal Highness, acting in the name and on the behalf of His Majesty, agrees, that the Naval Force to be maintained upon the American Lakes by His Majesty and the Government of the United States shall henceforth be confined to the following Vessels on each side—that is

On Lake Ontario to one Vessel not exceeding one hundred Tons burthen and armed with one eighteen pound cannon.

On the Upper Lakes to two Vessels not exceeding like burthen each and armed with like force.

On the waters of Lake Champlain to one Vessel not

exceeding like burthen and armed with like force.

And His Royal Highness agrees, that all other armed Vessels on these Lakes shall be forthwith dismantled, and that no other Vessels of War shall be there built or armed.

His Royal Highness further agrees, that if either Party should hereafter be desirous of annulling this Stipulation and should give notice to that effect to the other Party, it shall cease to be binding after the expiration of six months from the date of such notice.

The Undersigned has it in command from His Royal Highness the Prince Regent to acquaint the American Government, that His Royal Highness has issued orders to His Majesty's Officers on the Lakes directing, that the Naval Force so to be limited shall be restricted to such services as will in no respect interfere with the proper duties of the armed vessels of the other Party.

The Undersigned has the honour to renew to Mr. Rush the assurances of his highest consideration.

CHARLES BAGOT

EXCHANGE OF NOTES (FEBRUARY 26 AND MARCH 9, 1942) BETWEEN CANADA AND THE UNITED STATES OF AMERICA . . . IN FORCE MARCH 9, 1942 [18]

II

The Secretary of State for External Affairs, Ottawa, to the United States Minister to Canada.

Department of External Affairs

Ottawa, March 9, 1942

No. 21

Sir :—I have the honour to refer to your Note No. 611 dated 26th February, 1942, with regard to the further interpretation of the Rush-Bagot Agreement in the light of existing conditions and in conformity with the intent of the Agreement.

Consideration has been given to your suggestion, and I am now authorized to inform you that the Canadian Government agrees to a further interpretation of the Rush-Bagot Agreement based upon it. Accordingly, in order to

[18] Canada, *Treaty Series, 1942,* No. 3 (Ottawa, 1942), 4.

permit naval vessels being constructed on the Great Lakes to combat enemy action upon their arrival in the open sea, they will be permitted to have their armament placed in complete readiness for action and all essential tests and trials of machinery and armament including the submerged operations of submarines and test firing of torpedoes and guns may be effected in Great Lake waters.

The Canadian Government also concurs in your suggestion that this procedure should be effective only for the duration of the present hostilities.

Accept, Sir, the renewed assurances of my highest consideration.

N. A. ROBERTSON
for the Secretary of State for
External Affairs

— 18 —

THE FUR TRADE, 1833-1837 [19]

The fur trade has been a significant influence throughout the history of Canada. Its economic importance is obvious, but the trade also stimulated exploration, developed trade routes, transformed the life of the Indian, created a group of half-breeds, the Métis, determined the sites of cities, and put names on the map. In addition, the economic success of the fur trade did much to hold back settlement and thus delay the agricultural and industrial development of Canada.

[19] John McLean, *Notes of a Twenty-five Years' Service in the Hudson's Bay Territory* (London, 1849), I, 194-195, 306-308. A reprint of this work, edited by W. S. Wallace, was published by the Champlain Society, Toronto, in 1932, as volume XIX of their publications.

The fur trade produced a great body of literature. The documents given here were chosen because, though written by an ex-official of the Hudson's Bay Company, they are not official reports. Indeed, John McLean often was critical of the Company. His simply written narrative provides one of the richest storehouses of information on the fur trade from the inside at a critical time in its history. Since beavers for a long time were the monarchs of the fur bearers, the description of their trapping provides a valuable account of the first stage in the process of supplying furs to the European market. The document printed below gives also a good picture of the importance and the difficulties of the fur trade in New Caledonia, now part of the Province of British Columbia.

✤   ✤   ✤

. . . A good hunter always leaves his lodge by dawn of day, and seldom tastes food till he returns late at night. Hunting beavers is a most laborious occupation, and becomes more so in proportion to the scarcity of these animals; for this reason, that when a great number of beavers occupy a lake, their places of retreat are in closer proximity to each other, and for the most part inhabited; if the number be reduced, it is likely they will have the same places of retreat, and the hunter must bore through the ice, before he can ascertain whether they are inhabited or not.

The sagacity of their dogs is truly surprising. The beaver house being first destroyed by the hunter, the dogs are urged by a peculiar call to scent out their retreats, which they never fail to do, whatever may be the thickness of the ice. They keep running about the borders of the lake, their noses close to the ground, and the moment they discover a retreat, begin to bark and jump on the ice; the hunter then cuts a hole with his trench, and with a stick which he carries along with him feels for the beaver; should he find one, he introduces his bare arm into the hole, and seizing his prey by the tail, drags it out on the ice, where it is dispatched with a spear. There is less danger in this operation than one would imagine, for the beaver allows itself to be seized without a struggle, but sometimes inflicts severe wounds on his captor after he is taken out of the water.

When the retreat is not inhabited, the entrance to it is barred by sticks, and the hunter proceeds to chisel again, and continues his operations until the beaver is either taken, or shut out from all his haunts, in which case he is compelled to return to the house to take breath, where he is either shot or caught in a trap. . . .

New Caledonia is one of the richest districts in the Company's vast domain; its returns average about 8,000 beavers, with a fair proportion of other valuable furs. When the district was first settled, the goods required for trade were brought in by the winterers from Lac la Pluie, which was their dépôt. The people left the district as early in spring as the navigation permitted, and returned so late that they were frequently overtaken by winter ere they reached their destination. Cold, hunger, and fatigue, were the unavoidable consequences; but the enterprising spirit of the men of those days—the intrepid, indefatigable adventurers of the North-West Company—overcame every difficulty. It was that spirit that opened a communication across the broad continent of America; that penetrated to the frost-bound regions of the Arctic circle; and that established a trade with the natives in this remote land, when the merchandise required for it was in one season transported from Montreal to within a short distance of the Pacific. Such enterprise has never been exceeded, seldom or never equalled. The outfit is now sent out from England by Cape Horn, to Fort Vancouver, thence it is conveyed in boats to Okanagan, then transported on horses' backs to Alexandria, the lower post of the district, whence it is conveyed in boats to Fort St. James.

There are generally two commissioned gentlemen in this district,—a chief-factor and chief-trader, with six or seven clerks in charge of posts; and about forty men, principally Iroquois and half-breeds. The fare at the different posts depends entirely on local circumstances. In some places it is tolerable, in others, scarcely fit for dogs. For the year's consumption, the Company allow a clerk two bags of flour, sixty pounds of sugar, twelve pounds of tea, and a small quantity of wine and brandy. Butter is now produced in abundance in the district. Where there are no gardens, the men have only dried salmon,—as poor fare as civilized man subsists on in any part of the world. It has at first the same effect on most people as if they fed on Glauber salts. Nevertheless, the men generally continue in this wretched condition for many years, apparently contented and happy; the indulgence they find among the females being, I grieve to say, the principal inducement.

— 19 —

LORD DURHAM'S REPORT, FEBRUARY 11, 1839[20]

Armed rebellion was precipitated in Lower and Upper Canada in 1837 by a number of factors, such as the independent spirit of the frontier, inadequate machinery of government, and inept administration. A few abortive uprisings drew attention to the need for investigation and resulted in the appointment of the Earl of Durham as Commander-in-Chief of all the British North American provinces, except Newfoundland, High Commissioner for special purposes in Upper and Lower Canada, and Governor-General of all British North America. Durham's great report, although at first not acceptable, is significant as it charted the course of future British colonial policy. The full report was presented to the House of Commons on February 11, 1839, after The Times, *London, had re-*

[20] *Report on the Affairs of British North America from the Earl of Durham, Her Majesty's High Commissioner, &c. &c.&c.* Ordered by the House of Commons to be Printed, 11 February, 1839. Reprinted in *Appendix to Journal of the House of Assembly of Upper Canada, Session 1839* (Toronto, 1839), I, 3, 5, 89-92, 98-100.

vealed some of its contents, without the knowledge of Durham, on February 8.

✓   ✓   ✓

. . . While the present state of things is allowed to last, the actual inhabitants of these Provinces have no security for person or property, no enjoyment of what they possess, no stimulus to industry. . . .

The quarrel which I was sent for the purpose of healing, had been a quarrel between the executive government and the popular branch of the legislature. The latter body had, apparently, been contending for popular rights and free government. The executive government had been defending the prerogative of the Crown, and the institutions which, in accordance with the principles of the British Constitution, had been established as checks on the unbridled exercise of popular power. Though, during the dispute, indications had been given of the existence of dissensions yet deeper and more formidable than any which arose from simply political causes, I had still, in common with most of my countrymen, imagined that the original and constant source of the evil was to be found in the defects of the political institutions of the provinces; that a reform of the constitution, or perhaps merely the introduction of a sounder practice into the administration of the government, would remove all causes of contest and complaint. . . .

The preceding pages have sufficiently pointed out the nature of those evils, to the extensive operation of which, I attribute the various practical grievances, and the present unsatisfactory condition of the North American colonies. It is not by weakening, but strengthening the influence of the people on its government; by confining within much narrower bounds than those hitherto allotted to it, and not by extending the interference of the Imperial authorities in the details of colonial affairs, that I believe that harmony is to be restored, where dissension has so long prevailed; and a regularity and vigour hitherto unknown, introduced into the administration of these provinces. It needs no change in the pinciples of government, no invention of a new constitutional theory, to supply the remedy which would, in my opinion, completely remove the existing political disorders. It needs but to follow out consistently the principles of the British constitution, and introduce into the government of these great colonies those wise provisions, by which alone the working of the representative system can in any country be rendered harmonious and efficient. We are not now to consider the policy of establishing representative government in the North American colonies. That has been irrevocably done; and the experiment of depriving the people of their present constitutional power, is not to be thought of. To conduct their government harmoniously, in accordance with its established principles, is now the business of its rulers; and I know not how it is possible to secure that harmony in any other way, than by administering the government on those principles which have been found perfectly efficacious in Great Britain. I would not impair a single prerogative of the Crown; on the contrary, I believe that the interests of the people of these colonies require the protection of prerogatives, which have not hitherto been exercised. But the Crown must, on the other hand, submit to the necessary consequences of representative institutions: and if it has to carry on the government in unison with a representative body, it must consent to carry it on by means of those in whom that representative body has confidence.

In England this principle has been so long considered an indisputable and essential part of our constitution, that it has really hardly ever been found necessary to inquire into the means by which its observance is enforced. When a ministry ceases to command a majority in parliament on great questions of policy, its doom is immediately sealed; and it would appear to us as strange to attempt, for any time, to carry on a government by means of ministers perpetually in a minority, as it would be to pass laws with a majority of votes against them. The ancient constitutional remedies, by impeachment and a stoppage of the supplies, have never, since the reign of William III. been brought into operation for the purpose of removing a ministry. They have never been called for, because, in fact, it has been the habit of ministers rather to anticipate the occurrence of an absolutely hostile vote, and to retire, when supported only by a bare and uncertain ma-

jority. If colonial legislatures have frequently stopped the
supplies, if they have harassed public servants by unjust
or harsh impeachments, it was because the removal of an
unpopular administration could not be effected in the colonies by those milder indications of a want of confidence,
which have always sufficed to attain the end in the mother
country. . . .

I admit that the system which I propose would, in fact,
place the internal government of the colony in the hands
of the colonists themselves; and that we should thus leave
to them the execution of the laws, of which we have long
entrusted the making solely to them. Perfectly aware of
the value of our colonial possessions, and strongly im-
pressed with the necessity of maintaining our connexion
with them, I know not in what respect it can be desirable
that we should interfere with their internal legislation in
matters which do not affect their relations with the mother
country. The matters, which so concern us, are very few.
The constitution of the form of government—the regulation of foreign relations, and of trade with the mother
country, the other British colonies, and foreign nations,
and the disposal of the public lands, are the only points on
which the mother country requires a control. This control is now sufficiently secured by the authority of the Imperial legislature; by the protection which the colony
derives from us against foreign enemies; by the beneficial
terms which our laws secure to its trade; and by its share
of the reciprocal benefits which would be conferred by a
wise system of colonization. A perfect subordination on
the part of the colony on these points, is secured by the
advantages which it finds in the continuance of its connexion with the empire. It certainly is not strengthened,
but greatly weakened, by a vexatious interference on the
part of the home government, with the enactment of laws
for regulating the internal concerns of the colony, or in
the selection of the persons entrusted with their execution.
The colonists may not always know what laws are best
for them, or which of their countrymen are the fittest for
conducting their affairs; but, at least, they have a greater
interest in coming to a right judgment on these points,
and will take greater pains to do so, than those whose
welfare is very remotely and slightly affected by the good

or bad legislation of these portions of the empire. If the colonists make bad laws, and select improper persons to conduct their affairs, they will generally be the only, always the greatest, sufferers; and, like the people of other countries, they must bear the ills which they bring on themselves, until they choose to apply the remedy. . . .

The establishment of a good system of municipal institutions throughout these provinces is a matter of vital importance. A general legislature, which manages the private business of every parish, in addition to the common business of the country, wields a power which no single body, however popular in its constitution, ought to have—a power which must be destructive of any constitutional balance. The true principle of limiting popular power is that apportionment of it in many different depositaries, which has been adopted in all the most free and stable states of the Union. Instead of confiding the whole collection and distribution of all the revenues raised in any country for all general and local purposes to a single representative body, the power of local assessment, and the application of the funds arising from it, should be entrusted to local management. It is in vain to expect that this sacrifice of power will be voluntarily made by any representative body. The establishment of municipal institutions for the whole country should be made a part of every colonial constitution, and the prerogative of the crown should be constantly interposed to check any encroachment on the functions of the local bodies, until the people should become alive, as most assuredly they almost immediately would be, to the necessity of protecting their local privileges. . . .

I believe that no permanent or efficient remedy can be devised for the disorders of Lower Canada, except a fusion of the government in that of one or more of the surrounding provinces; and as I am of opinion that the full establishment of responsible government can only be permanently secured by giving these colonies an increased importance in the politics of the empire, I find in union the only means of remedying at once and completely the two prominent causes of their present unsatisfactory condition. . . .

I believe that tranquillity can only be restored by subjecting the province to the vigorous rule of an English majority; and that the only efficacious government would be that formed by a legislative union. . . .

But while I convince myself that such desirable ends would be secured by the legislative union of the two provinces, I am inclined to go further, and inquire whether all these objects would not more surely be attained, by extending this legislative union over all the British Provinces in North America; and whether the advantages which I anticipate for two of them might not, and should not, in justice be extended over all. Such an union would at once decisively settle the question of races; it would enable all the provinces to co-operate for all common purposes; and, above all, it would form a great and powerful people, possessing the means of securing good and responsible government for itself, and which, under the protection of the British empire, might in some measure counterbalance the preponderant and increasing influence of the United States on the American continent. I do not anticipate that a colonial legislature thus strong and thus self-governing, would desire to abandon the connexion with Great Britain. On the contrary, I believe that the practical relief from undue interference, which would be the result of such a change, would strengthen the present bond of feelings and interests; and that the connexion would only become more durable and advantageous, by having more of equality, of freedom, and of local independence. But, at any rate, our first duty is to secure the well-being of our colonial countrymen; and if in the hidden decrees of that wisdom by which this world is ruled, it is written, that these countries are not for ever to remain portions of the empire, we owe it to our honour to take good care that, when they separate from us, they should not be the only countries on the American continent in which the Anglo-Saxon race shall be found unfit to govern itself. . . .

— 20 —

A TRANSATLANTIC STEAMSHIP LINE, JULY 17, 1840[21]

*Available means of communication provide a useful in-
dication of the development of a nation. By this measure,
Canada went forward early in the 19th century for she led
the way in the use of steam for the propulsion of ocean-
going vessels. The* Royal William, *built in Quebec in
1831, though not designed for transatlantic service,
crossed the Atlantic from Pictou, Nova Scotia, to London,
propelled by steam and manned by a Canadian crew, in
August, 1833. Of greater significance was the establishment of a line of steamships operating on a regular schedule between England and Nova Scotia. Thanks largely to
the representations of Joseph Howe and Judge T. C. Hali-
burton, the British Admiralty in October, 1838, advertised
for tenders to carry mail by steamship between Liverpool,
Halifax, and Boston. A company newly organized by
Samuel Cunard, a Nova Scotian of Loyalist stock from
Pennsylvania, won the contract. The British and North
American Royal Mail Steam-Packet Company, as it was
called, immediately began building four ships of much the
same design. The* Britannia *was the first of the four to
cross, and her arrival, not unnaturally, caused great ex-
citement in Halifax and later in Boston. The following
extracts from contemporary Halifax newspapers reveal
something of the significance of the event.*

❧   ❧   ❧

ARRIVAL OF THE BRITANNIA

UNEXAMPLED LATENESS OF NEWS FROM ENGLAND.—At a
very early hour yesterday morning the elegant, new

[21] *Acadian Recorder,* July 18, 1840, and the *Nova Scotian,*
July 23, 1840.

steamship *Britannia* came up the harbor. She left Liverpool on the 4th instant, at half-past 2 p.m. and arrived here at 2 a.m. thus making the passage, in spite of head winds the whole time, in 299½ hours, or less, by half an hour, than 12½ days. She has brought 53 passengers, and among the number we are happy to congratulate His Lordship the Bishop of Nova Scotia and family, and the Hon. S. Cunard on their return to "Sweet Home." Mr. Featherstonhaugh also is one of the passengers.

A pilot was taken on board off Scatarie on Thursday, and although her arrival was generally looked for since Monday last, yet her appearance excited surprise as much as if she had come unexpectedly.

She is built long and narrow, and there seems to be a felicitous combination of grandeur, elegance, speed, and durability in her construction and *material*. She has a saloon, very tastefully furnished, on the deck, in which are two dining tables sufficiently large, we believe, to accommodate four hundred people. She is propelled by two sets of paddles, and her spars and rigging very much enhance her beauty.

We experienced much disappointment and delay in procuring papers; publishers in Boston and New York are accommodated immediately on the arrival of news with papers in abundance, and they are not subjected even to the trouble of seeking for them; they act upon a system of reciprocity; ours is one of indifference and selfishness.— *Acadian Recorder*

THE BRITANNIA.—The first of Mr. Cunard's regular line of Atlantic Steamships, arrived last Friday morning at half-past 2 o'clock. Public expectation was much excited for some days previous, and some feelings of disappointment and mortification were indulged, under the supposition that she left England on the 1st, and therefore failed to perform the voyage in due time. It is too much, perhaps, under any circumstances, to expect extreme regularity in any work of art, moving over a watery expanse of 3,000 miles. The many causes of difficulty and delay, incidental to such a road, should be taken into account, and make us reasonable and humble in our requirements. There was no excuse for any degree of complaint, however, respecting the *Britannia*'s first trip. She did not leave until the 4th, and arrived on the 17th, performing her arduous task, under some disadvantages of weather, and with new machinery, in 12 days and a half. This is all that could be desired, yet we understand that it is not all that may be expected, and that her captain says, he will accomplish the passage out in a day less, and home in ten days! It may be so, but 12 days may well be considered as a minimum, which is scarcely susceptible of diminution, and of which diminution should scarcely be wished. He who is not satisfied with travelling, steadily, 250 miles in a natural day, scarcely deserves satisfaction.

The *Britannia* left the wharf at 9 o'clock, went round *H.M.S. Winchester,* which was decorated with flags, and took the departure for Boston, under salutes of cannon.

She is a noble looking ship, fitted up, we understand in a comfortable, efficient, but plain style. . . .

Many preparations had been made to give the *Britannia* an enthusiastic reception in Boston. A public dinner, and various other festive demonstrations had been arranged, and service of plate was to be presented to Mr. Cunard, as a testimonial of the sense which the Bostonians entertain of his services.—The *Nova Scotian*

— 21 —

THE ACT OF UNION, JULY 23, 1840[22]

By 1840 financial difficulties in Upper Canada eased the way for the Imperial Parliament to join Upper and Lower

[22] 3-4 Victoria, c. 35. An Act to Re-unite the Provinces of *Upper* and *Lower Canada,* and for the Government of *Canada. The Provincial Statutes of Canada* (Kingston, 1841), I, iii-xxiv.

*Canada in a legislative union, as Lord Durham had rec-
ommended. The provisions for representation, however,
differed from Durham's proposals and ultimately caused
trouble.*

✓   ✓   ✓

Whereas it is necessary that Provision be made for the
good Government of the Provinces of *Upper Canada* and
Lower Canada, in such Manner as may secure the Rights
and Liberties and promote the Interests of all Classes of
Her Majesty's Subjects within the same: And whereas
to this end it is expedient that the said Provinces be re-
united and form One Province for the Purposes of Executive Government and Legislation; Be it therefore enacted
. . . That it shall be lawful for Her Majesty, with the
Advice of Her Privy Council, to declare, or to authorize
the Governor General of the said Two Provinces of *Upper*
and *Lower Canada* to declare, by Proclamation, that the
said Provinces, upon, from, and after a certain Day in
such Proclamation to be appointed, which Day shall be
within Fifteen Calendar Months next after the passing of
this Act, shall form and be One Province, under the
name of the Province of *Canada,* and thenceforth the said
Provinces shall constitute and be One Province, under the
name aforesaid, upon, from, and after the Day so appointed as aforesaid. . . .

III. And be it enacted, That from and after the Re-
union of the said Two Provinces there shall be within the
Province of *Canada* One Legislative Council and One
Assembly . . . which shall be called "The Legislative
Council and Assembly of *Canada;*" . . .

IV. And be it enacted, That for the Purpose of composing the Legislative Council of the Province of *Canada*
it shall be lawful for Her Majesty, before the Time to be
appointed for the First Meeting of the said Legislative
Council and Assembly, . . . to authorize the Governor, in
Her Majesty's Name, . . . to summon to the said Legislative Council of the said Province such Persons, being
not fewer than Twenty, as Her Majesty shall think fit;
and that it shall also be lawful for Her Majesty from
Time to Time to authorize the Governor in like Manner

to summon to the said Legislative Council such other Person or Persons as Her Majesty shall think fit, . . .

V. And be it enacted, That every Member of the Legislative Council of the Province of *Canada* shall hold his Seat therein for the Term of his Life, but subject nevertheless to the Provisions hereinafter contained for vacating the same.

VI. And be it enacted, That it shall be lawful for any Member of the Legislative Council of the Province of *Canada* to resign his Seat in the said Legislative Council, and upon such Resignation the Seat of such Legislative Councillor shall become vacant.

VII. And be it enacted, That if any Legislative Councillor of the Province of *Canada* shall for Two successive Sessions . . . fail to give his Attendance . . . without the Permission of Her Majesty or of the Governor, . . . or adopt any Act whereby he may become a Subject or Citizen of any Foreign State or Power, . . . or shall become bankrupt, . . . or become a public Defaulter, or be attainted of Treason, or be convicted of Felony or of any infamous Crime, his Seat . . . shall thereby become vacant. . . .

XI. And be it enacted, That for the Purpose of constituting the Legislative Assembly of the Province of *Canada* it shall be lawful for the Governor of the said Province, within the Time hereinafter mentioned, and thereafter from Time to Time as Occasion shall require, in Her Majesty's name, and by an Instrument or Instruments under the Great Seal of the said Province, to summon and call together a Legislative Assembly in and for the said Province.

XII. And be it enacted, That in the Legislative Assembly of the Province of *Canada* to be constituted as aforesaid the parts of the said Province which now constitute the Provinces of *Upper* and *Lower Canada* respectively shall, subject to the Provisions hereinafter contained, be represented by an equal number of Representatives, to be elected for the Places and in the Manner hereinafter mentioned. . . .

XXV. And be it enacted, That it shall be lawful for the Governor of the Province of *Canada* for the Time be-

ing to fix the Time and Place of holding Elections of
Members to serve in the Legislative Assembly of the said
Province, until otherwise provided for as herein-after is
mentioned, giving not less than Eight Days Notice of such
Time and Place. . . .

XXVIII. And be it enacted, That no Person shall be
capable of being elected a Member of the Legislative
Assembly of the Province of *Canada* who shall not be
legally or equitably seised as of Free-hold, for his own
Use and Benefit, of Lands or Tenements held in Free and
Common Socage, or seised or possessed, for his own Use
and Benefit, of Lands or Tenements held in Fief or in
Roture, within the said Province of *Canada,* of the Value
of Five hundred Pounds of Sterling Money of *Great
Britain,* over and above all Rents, Charges, Mortgages,
and Incumbrances charged upon and due and payable out
of or affecting the same ; . . .

XXX. And be it enacted, That it shall be lawful for
the Governor of the Province of *Canada* for the Time
being to fix such Place or Places within any Part of the
Province of *Canada,* and such Times for holding the First
and every other Session of the Legislative Council and
Assembly of the said Province as he may think fit, such
Times and Places to be afterwards changed or varied as
the Governor may judge advisable and most consistent
with general Convenience and the Public Welfare, giving
sufficient Notice thereof ; and also to prorogue the said
Legislative Council and Assembly from Time to Time,
and dissolve the same, by Proclamation or otherwise,
whenever he shall deem it expedient.

XXXI. And be it enacted, That there shall be a Session
of the Legislative Council and Assembly of the Province
of *Canada* once at least in every Year, so that a period
of Twelve Calendar Months shall not intervene between
the last Sitting of the Legislative Council and Assembly
in One Session and the First Sitting of the Legislative
Council and Assembly in the next Session ; and that every
Legislative Assembly of the said Province hereafter to be
summoned and chosen shall continue for Four Years from
the Day of the Return of the Writs for choosing the same,
and no longer, subject nevertheless to be sooner prorogued
or dissolved by the Governor of the said Province. . . .

XXXVIII. And be it enacted, That whenever any Bill which shall have been presented for Her Majesty's Assent to the Governor of the said Province of *Canada*, shall by such Governor have been assented to in Her Majesty's Name, such Governor shall, by the first convenient Opportunity, transmit to one of Her Majesty's Principal Secretaries of State an authentic Copy of Such Bill so assented to; and that it shall be lawful, at any Time within Two Years after such Bill shall have been so received by such Secretary of State, for Her Majesty, by Order in Council, to declare Her Disallowance of such Bill; . . .

— 22 —

THE ACHIEVEMENT OF RESPONSIBLE GOVERNMENT IN NOVA SCOTIA, 1848 [23]

Responsible government may be said to consist (1) in the Governor's choosing as executive advisers those who can command the confidence of the majority in the assembly and, consequently, represent the will of the electorate; and (2) in acting on the advice of these chosen advisers. The idea of responsible government in Canada occupied many minds and crystallized over many years. Robert Baldwin, of Upper Canada (Canada West), and Joseph Howe, of Nova Scotia, were among its leading proponents. It was in Nova Scotia that the first practical

[23] Earl Grey, *The Colonial Policy of Lord John Russell's Administration* (London, 1853), I, 209-213. Reprinted in A. G. Doughty, ed., *The Elgin-Grey Papers 1846-1852* (Ottawa, 1937), III, 1022-1023.

*application of the principle was made. Earl Grey, the
British Colonial Secretary, on November 3, 1846, wrote
to Sir John Harvey, Lieutenant-Governor of Nova Scotia,
outlining the general constitutional principles under which
he should act. Harvey did not carry out Grey's instructions immediately, but when a provincial election in 1847
resulted in a decisive victory for the Liberals, he bowed
to the will of the majority and on February 2, 1848, organized a responsible government in Nova Scotia. The
achievement of responsible government must be recognized as one of the most significant episodes in Canadian
political development. The policy of 1846 made it possible
to hold the diverse elements of the British Empire within
the framework of the British Commonwealth of Nations.*

*Lord Elgin, Governor-General of Canada, did not leave
Britain until January, 1847. Consequently, Earl Grey was
able to show him the principles which had been laid down
in the November 3, 1846, dispatch to Harvey. The most
significant paragraphs are those which Grey himself submitted to Elgin for comment. They are reproduced here.*

✓   ✓   ✓

I am of opinion that under all the circumstances of the
case, the best course for you to adopt is to call upon the
Members of your present Executive Council to propose to
you the names of the gentlemen whom they would recommend to supply the vacancies which I understand to exist
in the present Board.—If they should be successful in
submitting to you an arrangement to which no valid objection arises, you will of course continue to carry on the
Gov^t through them, so long as it may be possible to do so
satisfactorily, & as they possess the necessary support of
the Legislature.—Should the present Council fail in proposing to you an arrangement which it would be proper
for you to accept, it would then be your natural course, in
conformity with the practice of analogous cases in this
country, to apply to the opposite party, & should you be
able, through their assistance to form a satisfactory Council, there will be no impropriety in dissolving the Assembly upon their advice; such a measure under those
circumstances, being the only mode of escaping from the
difficulty which would otherwise exist of carrying on the

government of the province upon the principles of the constitution. The object with which I recommend to you this course, is that of making it apparent that any transfer which may take place of political power from the hands of one party in the province to those of another is the result not of an act of yours but of the wishes of the people themselves, as shown by the difficulty experienced by the retiring party in carrying on the government of the province according to the forms of the Constitution. To this I attach great importance; I have therefore to instruct you to abstain from changing your Executive Council until it shall become perfectly clear that they are unable, with such fair support from yourself as they have a right to expect, to carry on the government of the province satisfactorily, & command the confidence of the Legislature.

Of whatever party your Council may be composed, it will be your duty to act strictly upon the principle you have yourself laid down in the memorandum delivered to the gentlemen with whom you have communicated, that, namely, "of not identifying yourself with any one party" but instead of this, "making yourself both a mediator & moderator between the influential of all parties." In giving, therefore, all fair & proper support to your council for the time being, you will carefully avoid any acts which can possibly be supposed to imply the slightest personal objection to their opponents, & also refuse to assent to any measures which may be proposed to you by your Council which may appear to you to involve an improper exercise of the authority of the Crown for party rather than for public objects. In exercising, however this power of refusing to sanction measures which may be submitted to you by your Council, you must recollect that this power of opposing a check upon extreme measures proposed by the party for the time in the Gov^t depends entirely for its efficacy upon its being used sparingly, & with the greatest possible discretion. A refusal to accept advice tendered to you by your Council is a legitimate ground for its members to tender to you their resignation, a course they would doubtless adopt should they feel that the subject on which a difference had arisen between you & themselves was one upon which public opinion would

be in their favour.—Should it prove to be so, concession
to their views, must, sooner or later, become inevitable,
since it cannot be too distinctly acknowledged that it is
neither possible nor desirable to carry on the government
of any of the British provinces in North America in opposition to the opinion of the inhabitants.—Clearly understanding, therefore, that refusing to accede to the advice
of your council for the time being upon a point on which
they consider it their duty to insist, must lead to the question at issue being brought ultimately under the decision
of public opinion, you will carefully avoid allowing any
matter not of very grave concern, or upon which you
cannot reasonably calculate upon being in the end supported by that opinion to be made the subject of such a
difference.—And if, unfortunately, such a difference
should arise, you will take equal care that its cause, & the
grounds of your own decision are made clearly to appear
in written documents capable of being publicly quoted.—

The adoption of this principle of action by no means
involves the necessity of a blind obedience to the wishes &
opinions of the members of your Council; on the contrary,
I have no doubt that if they see clearly that your conduct
is guided, not by personal favour to any particular men
or party, but by a sincere desire to promote the public
good, your objections to any measures proposed will have
great weight with the Council, or should they prove un-
reasonable, with the Assembly, or in last resort, with the
public.—

Such are the general principles upon which the constitutions granted to the North American Colonies render it
necessary that their government should be conducted. . . .

— 23 —

THE ACHIEVEMENT OF RESPONSIBLE GOVERNMENT IN CANADA, 1849[24]

Nova Scotia achieved responsible government peaceably in 1848. The change did not come as smoothly in Canada. Lord Elgin, the Governor-General, knowing the policy of the British government, was prepared to apply the new principle. The opportunity came when a reform government, elected in January, 1848, passed a bill to compensate persons in Lower Canada who had suffered losses during the rebellion of 1837. The Tories complained that rebels were being compensated and shouted "Treason!" No matter what Elgin thought of the measure, he was convinced that he must sign it, which he did on April 25, 1849. A letter from Earl Grey, the British Colonial Secretary, confirmed Elgin in his opinion that he should accept rather than reserve the bill. His action precipitated riots in Montreal which culminated in the burning of the parliament buildings. A recently discovered letter from the Reverend W. R. Seaver, a Congregational minister, to his wife gives an eye-witness account of this episode.

✓ ✓ ✓

Montreal April 25th 1849

My dear Wife,
. . . Today the Govn came to town on horseback attended as usual by an aid and his Groom, went home about 3 o'clock and every one supposed the business of the day concluded and that his excellency had gone to dinner. But in about an hour more he came again to town *in state* at-

[24] Josephine Foster, "The Montreal Riot of 1849," *The Canadian Historical Review*, XXXII, 1951, 61-63.

tended by his officers and a Guard more than usually
numerous. What is all this about? was at once the in-
quiry. It was not supposed that it could be to give the
Royal Sanction to any bill, for before such a sanction is
given it is customary to give public notice to that effect
and call out the soldiers in front of Parliment house and
fire a salute with much more parade etc, but on this occasion there was no notice given and no display nor anything to indicate that the Royal Sanction was to be given
to any measure, but it was rumored that the Bill for in-
demnifying the Rebellion losses was now to be sanctioned
tho the members said it was the *New Tariff Bill,* but on
the report spreading thru town (which it did like wild-
fire) an immense mob assembled and sorounded the
Parliment house to see what his Excellency intended to
do—and when it was finally announced that he had really
given the Royal Sanction to the Bill, then there was
trouble—as his Excellency left the House for his carriage
at the door he was assailed with stones, clubs & rotten &
good eggs by thousands, and he was struck in the face
with an egg, his carriage windows broken etc, but by the
speed of his horses he was enabled to escape with no injury except to his carriage and his equipage—I stop here
for the cry is raised that the *Parliment House* is on fire—
fire—fire is the cry—and from my shop door I see the red
flames light up the Heavens—I go—more after I see
what the row is—

April 26th. Tis too true—Last night about 8 o'clock while
Parliment was still sitting a mob (it can be called nothing
else tho' composed of some of our most worthy citizens)
assembled around the House, and commenced the distruc-
tion of the building, by breaking windows etc. Soon the
doors were broken open and a stout fellow sprang into
the speakers chair with the exclamation *"I disolve Parliment"* This was the Signal—and immediately in the face
of the members, and an immense multitude of spectators
the Gas Pipes were fired in a dozen places, and the building wraped in flames—the "Golden Mace," sacred emblem
of Royalty, was seized by the infuriated mob and borne
into the street amid shouts of derision & scorn. The
Members barely escaped with their lives, and that splendid
Building with its rare paintings, all the records of the

Provinces from the first settlement, all the acts of Parliment, that Library, worth alone, £100,000, all, all, are distroyed. That splendid portrait of the Queen, which you may remember was droped into the street, and torn into a thousand pieces, All was lost, nothing saved, and the structure now is but a heap of smoking ruins. The loss to the city cannot be less than £300,000. The fire engines were not allowed to play upon the fire at all, and it was only on the arrival of General Gore with a body of soldiers that the engines were allowed to approach for the protection of other property. . . .

— 24 —

JOSEPH HOWE'S VISION OF CANADA, MAY 15, 1851 [25]

The 1850's in Canada saw a great development of railroads. Joseph Howe of Nova Scotia, however, had a vision far beyond that of most of his contemporaries. A Loyalist, born in Halifax of antecedents who had migrated to Massachusetts in the 17th century, Joseph Howe was a journalist, politician and orator. He led the campaign which ultimately resulted in the granting of responsible government to Nova Scotia in 1847. He spoke on many subjects (his speeches fill two large volumes), but probably his greatest speech was that delivered at Mason's Hall, Halifax, on May 15, 1851, extracts of which are given below. Lord Elgin wrote to Howe that he considered this speech one of the best that he had ever read.

[25] William Annand, ed., *The Speeches and Public Letters of the Hon. Joseph Howe* (Boston, 1858), II, 58-61.

✓   ✓   ✓

Mr. Mayor and Gentlemen,—This meeting has been called to ascertain whether the citizens of Halifax, after six months' deliberation and reflection, are as unanimous as they were in August last; whether they are still disposed to intrust to their government the task of constructing intercolonial railways; and whether they are prepared to accept the terms which have been offered to the Province in Mr. Hawes's letter of the 10th March. . . . I am happy in the belief that the unanimity which presages success, the manly forbearance and generous rivalry which insure the perfection of large and comprehensive measures upon sound principles do exist among us; do pervade the community, actuating and animating the large and highly respectable body of our fellow citizens here assembled. . . .

The imperial government, with a magnanimity which does honor to the British people, sustained by that unanimity of sentiment among the great leaders of public opinion at home which promises a long continuance of the honorable relations existing between us, has offered to the three British North American Provinces seven millions of pounds sterling, at the lowest interest at which money can be obtained in the world. This money is offered for the purpose of enabling them to complete, in an incredibly short space of time, and with security and ease, great internal improvements which their advanced condition renders so desirable; which will bind them together into one prosperous community, animate them with new hopes and aspirations, and ultimately elevate them from the Colonial condition to that of a great and prosperous nation, in perpetual amity and friendship with those glorious islands to which we trace our origin, and to which, through this great boon, so much of our material prosperity will in all time to come be traced.

Halifax has been formed by nature, and selected by the dictates of sound policy, as a common terminus for these great intercolonial railways. Three hundred and thirty miles will connect us with Portland, and all the lines which interlace the American Republic and bind together the prosperous communities of the South and West. Six hundred and seventy miles more, opening up the central lands and settlements of New Brunswick, will not only connect us, as we originally contemplated, with Quebec and the St. Lawrence, but passing through one hundred and eighty miles of settlements on that noble river, will place us in communication with the populous city of Montreal, which will soon be in connection with Portland on the other side; the circle will be thus complete, and the chains of intercommunication established, easily accessible, by shorter lines, to all the rising towns and settlements which that wide circuit will embrace.

But when Montreal is reached, shall we stop there? Who can believe it? Who can think so lightly of the enterprise of Western Canada as to apprehend that she will not continue this iron road, link by link, till it skirts the shores of Ontario and Erie, and draws its tributary streams of traffic from the prolific regions of Simcoe, Superior, and Huron? Already municipalities are organizing and companies are forming to extend this railway for six hundred miles above Montreal. Once completed to that city, how will those interior lines advance, How many interests will combine for their extension? . . .

But, sir, daring as may appear the scope of this conception, high as the destiny may seem which it discloses for our children, and boundless as are the fields of honorable labor which it presents, another, grander in proportions, opens beyond; one which the imagination of a poet could not exaggerate, but which the statesman may grasp and realize, even in our own day. Sir, to bind these disjointed Provinces together by iron roads; to give them the homogeneous character, fixedness of purpose, and elevation of sentiment, which they so much require, is our first duty. But, after all, they occupy but a limited portion of that boundless heritage which God and nature have given to us and to our children. Nova Scotia and New Brunswick are but the frontage of a territory which includes four millions of square miles, stretching away behind and beyond them, to the frozen regions on the one side and to the Pacific on the other. Of this great section of the globe, all the Northern Provinces, including Prince Edward Island and Newfoundland, occupy but four hundred and eighty-six thousand square miles. The Hudson's

Bay territory includes two hundred and fifty thousand miles. Throwing aside the more bleak and inhospitable regions, we have a magnificent country between Canada and the Pacific, out of which five or six noble Provinces may be formed, larger than any we have, and presenting to the hand of industry, and to the eye of speculation, every variety of soil, climate, and resource. With such a territory as this to overrun, organize and improve, think you that we shall stop even at the western bounds of Canada? or even at the shores of the Pacific? Vancouver's Island, with its vast coal measures, lies beyond. The beautiful islands of the Pacific and the growing commerce of the ocean, are beyond. Populous China and the rich East, are beyond; and the sails of our children's children will reflect as familiarly the sunbeams of the South, as they now brave the angry tempests of the North. The maritime Provinces which I now address, are but the Atlantic frontage of this boundless and prolific region; the wharves upon which its business will be transacted, and beside which its rich argosies are to lie. Nova Scotia is one of these. Will you, then, put your hands unitedly, with order, intelligence, and energy, to this great work? . . . I am neither a prophet, nor a son of a prophet, yet I will venture to predict that in five years we shall make the journey hence to Quebec and Montreal, and home through Portland and St. John, by rail; and I believe that many in this room will live to hear the whistle of the steam engine in the passes of the Rocky Mountains, and to make the journey from Halifax to the Pacific in five or six days. With such objects in view,—with the means before us to open up one thousand miles of this noble territory; to increase its resources and lay bare its treasures, surely all petty jealousies and personal rivalries should stand rebuked; all minor questions of mere local interest should give way. . . .

— 25 —

RECIPROCITY TREATY, 1854[26]

When in the 1840's Britain reduced and finally removed duties on corn and timber, she deprived her colonies of their preference in the British market. As early as 1848 the Earl of Elgin, Governor-General of Canada, in an effort to aid the Canadian farmers, proposed that Britain enter into a treaty with the United States providing for joint navigation of the St. Lawrence River on condition that Canadian produce be admitted into the United States duty free. Elgin strongly maintained his stand and at one time wrote, "Unless the markets of the States be opened to Canadian products it is quite hopeless to attempt to maintain the connexion with Gt. Britain under the present system of Commercial Policy." [27] After lengthy negotiations in which Elgin played an important part, a treaty was signed on June 5, 1854, and proclaimed in the United States on September 11. The treaty achieved its purpose, but not as thoroughly as its proponents had anticipated. The United States terminated the treaty in 1866, an action which played no little part in promoting pro-confederation thinking in British North America.

✦   ✦   ✦

ARTICLE I. It is agreed by the high contracting parties that in addition to the liberty secured to the United States fishermen by the above-mentioned convention of October 20, 1818, of taking, curing, and drying fish on certain coasts of the British North American Colonies therein defined, the inhabitants of the United States shall have, in common with the subjects of Her Britannic

[26] Malloy, comp., *Treaties, Conventions, International Acts, Protocols and Agreements,* I, 668-672.
[27] Doughty, ed., *The Elgin-Grey Papers, 1846-1852,* I, 150, 319.

Majesty, the liberty to take fish of every kind, except shell-fish, on the sea coasts and shores, and in the bays, harbors, and creeks of Canada, New Brunswick, Nova Scotia, Prince Edward's Island, and of the several islands thereunto adjacent, without being restricted to any distance from the shore, with permission to land upon the coasts and shores of those colonies and the islands thereof, and also upon the Magdalen Islands, for the purpose of drying their nets and curing their fish; provided that, in so doing, they do not interfere with the rights of private property, or with British fishermen, in the peaceable use of any part of the said coast in their occupancy for the same purpose.

It is understood that the above-mentioned liberty applies solely to the sea fishery, and that the salmon and shad fisheries, and all fisheries in rivers and the mouths of rivers, are hereby reserved exclusively for British fishermen. . . .

ARTICLE II. It is agreed by the high contracting parties that British subjects shall have, in common with the citizens of the United States the liberty to take fish of every kind, except shell-fish, on the eastern sea-coasts and shores of the United States north of the 36th parallel of north latitude, and on the shores of the several islands thereunto adjacent, and in the bays, harbors, and creeks of the said sea-coast and shores of the United States and of the said islands, without being restricted to any distance from the shore, with permission to land upon the said coasts of the United States and of the islands aforesaid, for the purpose of drying their nets and curing their fish: Provided, that, in so doing, they do not interfere with the rights of private property, or with the fishermen of the United States, in the peaceable use of any part of the said coasts in their occupancy for the same purpose.

It is understood that the above-mentioned liberty applies solely to the sea fishery, and that salmon and shad fisheries, and all fisheries in rivers and mouths of rivers, are hereby reserved exclusively for fishermen of the United States.

ARTICLE III. It is agreed that the articles enumerated in the schedule hereunto annexed, being the growth and produce of the aforesaid British colonies or of the

United States, shall be admitted into each country respectively free of duty:

Schedule

Grain, flour, and breadstuffs, of all kinds.
Animals of all kinds.
Fresh, smoked, and salted meats.
Cotton-wool, seeds, and vegetables.
Undried fruits, dried fruits.
Fish of all kinds.
Products of fish, and of all other creatures living in the water.
Poultry, eggs.
Hides, furs, skins, or tails, undressed.
Stone or marble, in its crude or unwrought state.
Slate.
Butter, cheese, tallow.
Lard, horns, manures.
Ores of metals, of all kinds.
Coal.
Pitch, tar, turpentine, ashes.
Timber and lumber of all kinds, round, hewed, and sawed, unmanufactured in whole or in part.
Firewood.
Plants, shrubs, and trees.
Pelts, wool.
Fish-oil.
Rice, broom-corn, and bark.
Gypsum, ground or unground.
Hewn, or wrought, or unwrought burr or grindstones.
Dyestuffs.
Flax, hemp, and tow, unmanufactured.
Unmanufactured tobacco.
Rags.

ARTICLE IV. It is agreed that the citizens and inhabitants of the United States shall have the right to navigate the River St. Lawrence, and the canals in Canada used as the means of communicating between the great lakes and the Atlantic Ocean, with their vessels, boats, and crafts, as fully and freely as the subjects of Her Britannic Majesty, subject only to the same tolls and other assessments as now are, or may hereafter be, exacted of Her Majesty's said subjects; it being understood, however, that the British Government retains the right of suspending this privilege on giving due notice thereof to the Government of the United States. . . .

It is further agreed that British subjects shall have the right freely to navigate Lake Michigan with their vessels, boats, and crafts so long as the privilege of navigating the river St. Lawrence, secured to American citizens by the above clause of the present article, shall continue; and the Government of the United States further engages to urge upon the State governments to secure to the subjects of Her Britannic Majesty the use of the several State canals on terms of equality with the inhabitants of the United States.

And it is further agreed that no export duty, or other duty, shall be levied on lumber or timber of any kind cut on that portion of the American territory in the State of Maine watered by the river St. John and its tributaries, and floated down that river to the sea, when the same is shipped to the United States from the province of New Brunswick.

ARTICLE V. The present treaty shall take effect as soon as the laws required to carry it into operation shall have been passed by the Imperial Parliament of Great Britain and by the Provincial Parliaments of those of the British North American colonies which are affected by this treaty on the one hand, and by the Congress of the United States on the other. Such assent having been given, the treaty shall remain in force for ten years from the date at which it may come into operation, and further until the expiration of twelve months after either of the high contracting parties shall give notice to the other of its wish to terminate the same; each of the high contracting parties being at liberty to give such notice to the other at the end of the said term of ten years, or at any time afterwards. . . .

ARTICLE VI. And it is hereby further agreed that the provisions and stipulations of the foregoing articles shall extend to the island of Newfoundland, so far as they are applicable to that colony. But if the Imperial Parliament, the Provincial Parliament of Newfoundland, or the Congress of the United States shall not embrace in their laws, enacted for carrying this treaty into effect, the colony of Newfoundland, then this article shall be of no effect; but the omission to make provision by law to give it effect, by either of the legislative bodies aforesaid, shall not in any way impair the remaining articles of this treaty.

ARTICLE VII. The present treaty shall be duly ratified, and the mutual exchange of ratifications shall take place in Washington within six months from the date hereof, or earlier if possible.

In faith whereof we, the respective Plenipotentiaries, have signed this treaty and have hereunto affixed our seals.

Done in triplicate, at Washington, the fifth day of June, anno Domini one thousand eight hundred and fifty-four.

[Seal]   W. L. MARCY
[Seal]   ELGIN & KINCARDINE

— 26 —

CANADA'S INTEREST IN THE AMERICAN CIVIL WAR. AN ADDRESS DELIVERED DURING THE AGRICULTURAL EXHIBITION, AT LONDON, CANADA WEST, SEPTEMBER 26, 1861[28]

The American Civil War inevitably aroused great interest in the British North American Colonies. The strug-

---

[28] Thomas D'Arcy McGee, *Speeches and Addresses chiefly on the Subject of British-American Union* (London, 1865), 12-15, 24-25, 30-32.

gle ultimately played no small part in drawing the colonies together and dictating the form of the constitution.

An Irish immigrant into Canada in 1847, assassinated in 1868, Thomas D'Arcy McGee in ten years established himself as a leading journalist, orator, and statesman. He became the spokesman for the Confederation of 1867. The document printed below illustrates a vocal Canadian nationalist's view of the issues in the Civil War as far as they affected Canada.

. . . It was thought that we might spend an evening not unprofitably in considering how far we are likely to be affected in our peaceful progress, our domestic industry, and our external relations, by the stirring events which are taking place on the soil of Virginia and Missouri. Our friends were of opinion—and I fully agree with them—that while cultivating our own fields in peace, under the broad banner of the triple cross—that while cherishing with a natural preference our own institutions, copied in general after the model furnished by our Island ancestors, we still cannot be insensible to the revolution attempted to the south of those great lakes, upon which a portion of Upper Canadians dwell and depend, and from which we in Lower Canada derive most of our freights and exchanges. Standing as we do to the north of the North, riding safely by the firm anchorage of a system of self-government, the most liberal that metropolis ever conceded to colony, since the emigrating ages of the Greeks—bound up with the fortunes of a great empire by "links light as air, yet strong as iron," we conceive that the public intelligence of Canada is sufficiently centred in itself, sufficiently calm, unbiassed, and comprehensive, to form opinions for ourselves, neither parrotted after the organs of the North, nor echoed after the orators of the South. . . . In Canada we have this advantage over both North and South, in their present blood-heat temper: we can express ourselves, without fear of censorship or Lynch Law, whenever we do see our way clearly, and feel that there is a principle at stake. While I feel buoyed up in an atmosphere of free speech, I must add, on the other hand, that I feel borne down

almost to speechlessness by the vastness of the subject.
. . . The interests of Canada in the American civil war
are, in general, the interest of all free governments, and
in particular the interest of a next neighbour, having a
thousand miles of frontier and many social enterprises in
common with the Republic. We are ourselves an American people geographically and commercially, though we
retain our British connection; our situation is continental,
and our politics, in the largest and best sense, must needs
be continental. It is true our Federal capital is on the
other side of the Atlantic, not on this; but although subject to a constitutional monarchy in our external affairs,
we claim to be as free a people—indeed, we flatter ourselves we are a freer people—than our neighbours of New
York, or New England, or the North-western States. As
a free people, with absolute domestic self-government,
with local liberties, bound up in an Imperial Union, governed by our own majority constitutionally ascertained,
we are as deeply interested in the issue of the present unhappy contest, as any of the States of the United States;
while, as a North American people, Canadians are more
immediately and intimately concerned in the issue than
any other population, not excepting the West Indians or
the Mexicans. . . .

In the first stages of the contest, it seemed to me and
others, that the public sympathy in this country was altogether with the North. Some offensive bravado from
one or two New York newspapers was made use of by
some one or more Canadian journals, to arrest, to turn
back the genial currents of that sympathy. A pretence
was next made that it was a war undertaken from a lust
of dominion, and not from any sincere love of liberty. . . .

Another argument calculated to prejudice the Canadian
mind is this, that the Free are endeavouring to enforce
upon the Slave States the very same superiority which
their revolutionary fathers denied to Great Britain. If I
understand the merits of the American revolution, there
is no parallel whatever in the causes of quarrel. . . .

Whatever indirect advantage Canada or the Empire
might derive from the war, the people of Canada can
never be indifferent to the dangers to the system of free
intercourse and common arbiter, which is to stand or

fall in this encounter. It is not by feeding our minds with such paltry passions as have been sometimes appealed to, that we, the possessors of a seventh part of North America, are to shame our Republican neighbours out of their assaults upon ourselves. Our littleness is not to rebuke their littleness; we are not to answer railing with railing, nor to heap up wrath against the day of wrath. . . . We do not . . . while the ship is driving on the rocks, her signal gun pealing for aid above the din of the tempest—we do not lurk along the shore, gloating over her danger, in hope of enriching ourselves by the wreck. No, God forbid! Such is not the feeling of the people of Canada. On the contrary, so far as their public opinion can be heard throughout the British Empire or the United States, their wish would be that the Republic, as it was twelve months ago, might live to celebrate in concord, in 1876, the centenary of its Independence. We prefer our own institutions to theirs; but our preference is rational, not rancorous; we may think, and we do think, it would have been well for them to have retained more than they did retain of the long-tried wisdom of their ancestors; we may think, and we do think, that their overthrow of ancient precedents and venerable safeguards was too sweeping in 1776; but as between continental peace and chronic civil war—as between natural right and oligarchical oppression; as between the constitutional majority and the lawless minority; as between free intercourse and armed frontiers; as between negro emancipation and a revival of the slave trade; as between the golden rule and the cotton crop of 1861; as between the revealed unity of the race and the heartless heresy of African bestiality; as between the North and South in this deplorable contest, I rest firmly in the belief, that all that is most liberal, most intelligent, and most magnanimous in Canada and the Empire, are for continental peace, for constitutional arbitrament, for universal, if gradual emancipation, for free intercourse, for justice, mercy, civilisation, and the North.

— 27 —

THE GOLD DIGGINGS OF BRITISH COLUMBIA, 1862 [29]

Gold rushes are exciting, and the one to New Caledonia, or what is now the Province of British Columbia, in 1858, was no exception. The first rush to the Fraser River ended in a few months, but new discoveries further up the river and in the Cariboo in 1860-61 began a new rush. The search for gold had lasting effects in the country. The great influx of people, at first creating difficult problems of maintaining law and order, finally resulted in British Columbia's becoming a Canadian province in 1871, only thirteen years after the first rush.

Accounts written by participants are not numerous; fortune-seeking miners had something better to do than writing. Some of the few available records have been printed in The British Columbia Historical Quarterly, *which began publishing them in 1937. But since the experiences of a single participant do not give a general view, the document given below was chosen. It is the account of a qualified observer, a* Times *(London) correspondent.*

✦   ✦   ✦

Victoria, Vancouver's Island, Jan. 20, 1862

In my last letter I gave a detailed account of the mining operations in British Columbia during the season of 1861. In this letter I propose to give a general sketch of the mineral region with the view of conveying to such as have not been in the country a definite conception of the extent and capabilities of the goldfield.

[29] Printed in Henry Youle Hind, *A Sketch of an Overland Route to British Columbia* (Toronto, 1862), 119-121.

THE LOCALE OF THE GOLD DIGGINGS

Beginning with Fraser River, the main artery of the auriferous region, I may state that gold is known to exist and has been worked at a great many places in the river and on its banks from a point about 43 miles from the mouth of the river up to near its source in the Rocky Mountains; in other words, from the 40th up to the 53rd parallel of north latitude, a distance (taking in the windings) of some 800 miles. The south branch of the Fraser has its source near Mount Brown in the Rocky Mountains, in about 53° north latitude, 148° 40 min. west longitude. Thence this branch flows for 290 miles to Fort George, a post of the Hudson's Bay Company. The north branch rises in an opposite direction. It receives its supply from a series of lakes lying between 54° and 55° of north latitude, longitude about 124° 50 min. west, and runs a course 260 miles to its junction with the south branch, some miles below the 54th parallel of north latitude. Here the union of the two branches forms the Fraser River proper. Adding the north branch, which is also a gold bearing stream, and which was "worked" last season to the other arm, the two will give us a continuous stretch of auriferous riverain territory upwards of 1,009 miles in length, extending for many miles back into the country on both sides, but not including the tributary rivers which fall into the Fraser. In short, the river itself is now known to be auriferous and to pass through a gold bearing country throughout its whole course. Gold is also found in most of the tributaries of the Fraser, of which no less than 59 are known. The great length of the main river and the number of its tributaries will give some idea of the auriferous resources of the country.

THE TERRACES OF THE FRASER

But these facts do not by any means convey a comprehensive or accurate view of the vast extent of the area of the goldfield, because they are limited to the central portions of the country, while the whole of the upper portions of British Columbia, from its southern to its northern boundary, is auriferous. Besides the gold found in the beds and on the shores of these streams the Fraser

itself and many of its tributaries are skirted or bordered
by terraces, all of which yield gold also. . . .

Leaving the solution of their formation to the learned in
such matters, I will hasten to explain their value to the
miner. They contain vast deposits of gold; and to be
worked to advantage the "bench diggings" must command
a stream of water supplied from a source higher than
their own surfaces, so as to give a fall to enable the
miner to apply the water to the face of the "bench" by a
hose. The force of the stream is due to the height of the
fall. A good strong stream playing upon the face of the
hill will disintegrate a great quantity of "pay dirt" in a
short time. The floating rubbish, or "dirt," is caught in a
long sluice at the base, provided with "riffles" on the bot-
tom, and spread with quicksilver to catch the gold. This
mode of mining is called by the miners "hydraulic mining." Such is the wealth of Cariboo that no quicksilver
was used, for the miners could afford to loose all the "fine
dust" and to be satisfied with the "lumps." It happens
fortunately, that Fraser River and most of its tributaries
supply water in abundance at an elevation which affords
the necessary fall, from the elevated and broken character
of the country; while there are inexhaustible supplies in
the numerous lakes dispersed all over the upper district.
Timber for the erection of "flumes" is also abundant
everywhere. British Columbia is better supplied with water for mining purposes, obtainable both from streams at
great elevations, and from lakes situated in high altitudes,
than either California or Australia. Some of the "ditches"
in California are of great length; some 40 miles, owing to
the absence of streams running on elevated planes. The
cost of construction is consequently very great. But Australia is much worse off, for there is an actual scarcity of
water. The canal system of British Columbia will be comparatively inexpensive from the abundance of water and
its eligibility, encouraging facts to the miner, because the
small outlay of capital required will keep his "water dues"
low. . . .

— 28 —

JOHN A. MACDONALD ON CONFEDERATION, 1865 [30]

From 1854 to 1891 the figure of Sir John A. Mac-donald (knighted in 1867) towered over the Canadian political scene. To him must go most of the credit for drawing together the provinces which entered Confedera-tion in 1867, and for holding together and expanding the young nation. When the subject of Confederation was being debated in the Canadian Assembly it was Mac-donald who presented the motion, on February 6, 1865. In his speech on that occasion Macdonald gave a résumé of the background, and something of what he saw in store for the Dominion. His vision was prophetic. Confedera-tion was the prerequisite for the national development of Canada, and Macdonald's key contribution opened the way for the subsequent steps which culminated in complete autonomy.

*   *   *

. . . I have had the honor of being charged, on behalf of the Government, to submit a scheme for the Con-federation of all the British North American Provinces —a scheme which has been received, I am glad to say, with general, if not universal, approbation in Canada. . . . This subject, which now absorbs the attention of the people of Canada, and of the whole of British North America, is not a new one. For years it has more or less attracted the attention of every statesman and politician in these provinces, and has been looked upon by many far-seeing politicians as being eventually the means of deciding and settling very many of the vexed questions

---

[30] *Parliamentary Debates on the Subject of Confederation . . .* (Quebec, 1865), 25, 27-29, 32-33, 40, 43-45.

which have retarded the prosperity of the colonies as a whole, and particularly the prosperity of Canada. . . .

But the subject was not taken up by any party as a branch of their policy, until the formation of the Cartier-Macdonald Administration in 1858, when the Confederation of the colonies was announced as one of the measures which they pledged themselves to attempt, if possible, to bring to a satisfactory conclusion. . . . By a happy concurrence of events, the time came when that proposition could be made with a hope of success. By a fortunate coincidence the desire for union existed in the Lower Provinces, and a feeling of the necessity of strengthening themselves by collecting together the scattered colonies on the sea-board, had induced them to form a convention of their own for the purpose of effecting a union of the Maritime Provinces of Nova Scotia, New Brunswick, and Prince Edward Island, the legislatures of those colonies having formally authorized their respective governments to send a delegation to Prince Edward Island for the purpose of attempting to form a union of some kind. Whether the union should be federal or legislative was not then indicated, but a union of some kind was sought for the purpose of making of themselves one people instead of three. We, ascertaining that they were about to take such a step, and knowing that if we allowed the occasion to pass, if they did indeed break up all their present political organizations and form a new one, it could not be expected that they would again readily destroy the new organization which they had formed,—the union of the three provinces on the sea-board,—and form another with Canada. Knowing this, we availed ourselves of the opportunity, and asked if they would receive a deputation from Canada, who would go to meet them at Charlottetown, for the purpose of laying before them the advantages of a larger and more extensive union, by the junction of all the provinces in one great government under our common Sovereign. They at once kindly consented to receive and hear us. They did receive us cordially and generously, and asked us to lay our views before them. We did so at some length, and so satisfactory to them were the reasons we gave; so clearly, in their opinion, did we shew the advantages of the greater union over the lesser, that they at once set aside their own project, and joined heart and hand with us in entering into the larger scheme, and trying to form, as far as they and we could, a great nation and a strong government. (Cheers.)

Encouraged by this arrangement, which, however, was altogether unofficial and unauthorized, we returned to Quebec, and then the Government of Canada invited the several governments of the sister colonies to send a deputation here from each of them for the purpose of considering the question, with something like authority from their respective governments. The result was, that when we met here on the 10th of October, on the first day on which we assembled, after the full and free discussions which had taken place at Charlottetown, the first resolution now before this House was passed unanimously, being received with acclamation as, in the opinion of every one who heard it, a proposition which ought to receive, and would receive, the sanction of each government and each people. The resolution is, "That the best interests and present and future prosperity of British North America will be promoted by a Federal Union under the Crown of Great Britain, provided such union can be effected on principles just to the several provinces." It seemed to all the statesmen assembled—and there are great statesmen in the Lower Provinces, men who would do honor to any government and to any legislature of any free country enjoying representative institutions—it was clear to them all that the best interests and present and future prosperity of British North America would be promoted by a Federal Union under the Crown of Great Britain. And it seems to me, as to them, and I think it will so appear to the people of this country, that, if we wish to be a great people; if we wish to form—using the expression which was sneered at the other evening— a great nationality, commanding the respect of the world, able to hold our own against all opponents, and to defend those institutions we prize; if we wish to have one system of government, and to establish a commercial union, with unrestricted free trade, between people of the five provinces, belonging, as they do, to the same nation, obeying the same Sovereign, owning the same allegiance, and being, for the most part, of the same blood and lineage; if we wish to be able to afford to each other the means of mutual defence and support against aggression and attack—this can only be obtained by a union of some kind between the scattered and weak boundaries composing the British North American Provinces. (Cheers). . . .

Now, as regards the comparative advantages of a Legislative and a Federal Union, I have never hesitated to state my own opinions. I have again and again stated in the House, that, if practicable, I thought a Legislative Union would be preferable. . . . But, on looking at the subject in the Conference, and discussing the matter as we did, most unreservedly, and with a desire to arrive at a satisfactory conclusion, we found that such a system was impracticable. . . . The Conference having come to the conclusion that a legislative union, pure and simple, was impracticable, our next attempt was to form a government upon federal principles, which would give to the General Government the strength of a legislative and administrative union, while at the same time it preserved that liberty of action for the different sections which is allowed by a Federal Union. And I am strong in the belief—that we have hit upon the happy medium in those resolutions, and that we have formed a scheme of government which unites the advantages of both, giving us the strength of a legislative union and the sectional freedom of a federal union, with protection to local interests. In doing so we had the advantage of the experience of the United States. It is the fashion now to enlarge on the defects of the Constitution of the United States, but I am not one of those who look upon it as a failure. (Hear, hear.) I think and believe that it is one of the most skillful works which human intelligence ever created; is one of the most perfect organizations that ever governed a free people. To say that it has some defects is but to say that it is not the work of Omniscience, but of human intellects. We are happily situated in having had the opportunity of watching its operation, seeing its working from its infancy till now. . . . We can now take advantage of the experience of the last seventy-eight years, during which that Constitution has existed, and I am strongly of the belief that we have, in a great measure,

avoided in this system which we propose for the adoption
of the people of Canada, the defects which time and events
have shown to exist in the American Constitution. . . .

Ever since the union was formed the difficulty of what
is called "State Rights" has existed, and this had much
to do in bringing on the present unhappy war in the
United States. They commenced, in fact, at the wrong
end. They declared by their Constitution that each state
was a sovereignty in itself, and that all the powers incident to a sovereignty belonged to each state, except those
powers which, by the Constitution, were conferred upon
the General Government and Congress. Here we have
adopted a different system. We have strengthened the
General Government. We have given the General Legislature all the great subjects of legislation. We have conferred on them, not only specifically and in detail, all the
powers which are incident to sovereignty, but we have
expressly declared that all subjects of general interest not
distinctly and exclusively conferred upon the local governments and local legislatures, shall be conferred upon
the General Government and Legislature.—We have thus
avoided that great source of weakness which has been
the cause of the disruption of the United States. . . . I
shall not detain the House by entering into a consideration at any length of the different powers conferred upon
the General Parliament as contradistinguished from those
reserved to the local legislatures; but any honorable
member on examining the list of different subjects which
are to be assigned to the General and Local Legislatures
respectively, will see that all the great questions which
affect the general interests of the Confederacy as a whole,
are confided to the Federal Parliament, while the local
interests and local laws of each section are preserved
intact, and entrusted to the care of the local bodies. . . .

Let me again, before I sit down, impress upon this
House the necessity of meeting this question in a spirit of
compromise, with a disposition to judge the matter as a
whole, to consider whether really it is for the benefit and
advantage of the country to form a Confederation of all
the provinces; and if honorable gentlemen, whatever may
have been their preconceived ideas as to the merits of the
details of this measure, whatever may still be their opin-

ions as to these details, if they really believe that the scheme is one by which the prosperity of the country will be increased, and its future progress secured, I ask them to yield their own views, and to deal with the scheme according to its merits as one great whole. (Hear, hear.)

One argument, but not a strong one, has been used against this Confederation, that it is an advance towards independence. Some are apprehensive that the very fact of our forming this union will hasten the time when we shall be severed from the mother country. I have no apprehension of that kind. I believe it will have the contrary effect. I believe that as we grow stronger, that, as it is felt in England we have become a people, able from our union, our strength, our population, and the development of our resources, to take our position among the nations of the world, she will be less willing to part with us than she would be now, when we are broken up into a number of insignificant colonies, subject to attack piecemeal without any concerted action or common organization of defence. I am strongly of opinion that year by year, as we grow in population and strength, England will more see the advantages of maintaining the alliance between British North America and herself. Does any one imagine that, when our population instead of three and a-half, will be seven millions, as it will be ere many years pass, we would be one whit more willing than now to sever the connection with England? Would not those seven millions be just as anxious to maintain their allegiance to the Queen and their connection with the Mother Country, as we are now? . . . When this union takes place, we will be at the outset no inconsiderable people. We find ourselves with a population approaching four millions of souls. Such a population in Europe would make a second, or at least, a third rate power. And with a rapidly increasing population—for I am satisfied that under this union our population will increase in a still greater ratio than ever before—with increased credit—with a higher position in the eyes of Europe—with the increased security we can offer to immigrants, who would naturally prefer to seek a new home in what is known to them as a great country, than in any one little colony or another—with all this I am satisfied that, great as has been our increase in the last twenty-five years since the union between Upper and Lower Canada, our future progress, during the next quarter of a century, will be vastly greater. (Cheers.) And when, by means of this rapid increase, we become a nation of eight or nine millions of inhabitants, our alliance will be worthy of being sought by the great nations of the earth. (Hear, hear.) I am proud to believe that our desire for a permanent alliance will be reciprocated in England. . . .

The colonies are now in a transition state. Gradually a different colonial system is being developed—and it will become, year by year, less a case of dependence on our part, and of overruling protection on the part of the Mother Country, and more a case of a healthy and cordial alliance. Instead of looking upon us as a merely dependent colony, England will have in us a friendly nation—a subordinate but still a powerful people—to stand by her in North America in peace or in war. (Cheers.)

The people of Australia will be such another subordinate nation. And England will have this advantage, if her colonies progress under the new colonial system, as I believe they will, that, though at war with all the rest of the world, she will be able to look to the subordinate nations in alliance with her, and owning allegiance to the same Sovereign, who will assist in enabling her again to meet the whole world in arms, as she has done before. (Cheers.) . . . I must apologize for having detained you so long—for having gone perhaps too much into tedious details with reference to the questions bearing on the Constitution now submitted to this House.—(Cries of "no, no" and "go on.") . . .

In conclusion, I would again implore the House not to let this opportunity to pass. It is an opportunity that may never recur. At the risk of repeating myself, I would say, it was only by a happy concurrence of circumstances, that we were enabled to bring this great question to its present position. If we do not take advantage of the time, if we show ourselves unequal to the occasion, it may never return, and we shall hereafter bitterly and unavailingly regret having failed to embrace the happy opportunity now offered of founding a great nation under the fostering care of Great Britain, and our Sovereign Lady, Queen Victoria. (Loud cheers, amidst which the honorable gentleman resumed his seat.)

— 29 —

THE BRITISH NORTH AMERICA ACT, 1867[31]

Many factors combined to bring Canadian Confederation in 1867. Political deadlock in Canada and the temporary submerging of political animosities; the need to develop markets, particularly after the termination of the Reciprocity Treaty of 1854 by the United States in 1866; fear of American designs in the west, calling for a unified defence; the need for expansion to make use of railway facilities already built and the urge to build new ones; all played their part in creating an atmosphere favorable to union. But the feeling of destiny and the logic of the idea of Confederation which had often been expressed must be given a leading place among the causes. The legal document which brought about Confederation was the British North America Act, a statute of the Parliament of the United Kingdom. It received Royal Assent March 29, 1867. The first day of July, 1867, was fixed by proclamation as the day when the three uniting provinces should "form and be One Dominion." Sections 91 and 92, covering as they do the distribution of powers between the government of Canada and the governments of the provinces, are particularly important. They reveal a significant difference between the British North America Act and the

[31] *A Consolidation of the British North America Acts 1867 to 1952* (Ottawa, 1956).

Constitution of the United States, which the framers of the Canadian document had constantly in their minds.

✠   ✠   ✠

I.—PRELIMINARY

1. This Act may be cited as The British North America Act, 1867. . . .

II.—UNION

3. It shall be lawful for the Queen, by and with the Advice of Her Majesty's Most Honourable Privy Council, to declare by Proclamation that, on and after a Day therein appointed, not being more than Six months after the passing of this Act, the Provinces of Canada, Nova Scotia, and New Brunswick shall form and be One Dominion under the Name of Canada; and on and after that Day those Three Provinces shall form and be One Dominion under that Name accordingly. . . .

5. Canada shall be divided into Four Provinces, named Ontario, Quebec, Nova Scotia, and New Brunswick. . . .

III.—EXECUTIVE POWER

9. The Executive Government and Authority of and over Canada is hereby declared to continue and be vested in the Queen.

10. The Provisions of this Act referring to the Governor General extend and apply to the Governor General for the Time being of Canada, or other the Chief Executive Officer or Administrator for the Time being carrying on the Government of Canada on behalf and in the Name of the Queen, by whatever Title he is designated.

11. There shall be a Council to aid and advise in the Government of Canada, to be styled the Queen's Privy Council for Canada; and the Persons who are to be Members of that Council shall be from Time to Time chosen and summoned by the Governor General and sworn in as Privy Councillors, and Members thereof may be from Time to Time removed by the Governor General. . . .

16. Until the Queen otherwise directs, the Seat of Government of Canada shall be Ottawa.

IV.—LEGISLATIVE POWER

17. There shall be One Parliament for Canada, consisting of the Queen, an Upper House styled the Senate, and the House of Commons. . . .

50. Every House of Commons shall continue for Five Years from the Day of the Return of the Writs for choosing the House (subject to be sooner dissolved by the Governor General), and no longer. . . .

53. Bills for appropriating any Part of the Public Revenue, or for imposing any Tax or Impost, shall originate in the House of Commons.

54. It shall not be lawful for the House of Commons to adopt or pass any Vote, Resolution, Address, or Bill for the Appropriation of any Part of the Public Revenue, or of any Tax or Impost, to any Purpose that has not been first recommended to that House by Message of the Governor General in the Session in which such Vote, Resolution, Address, or Bill is proposed. . . .

VI.—DISTRIBUTION OF LEGISLATIVE POWERS

91. It shall be lawful for the Queen, by and with the Advice and Consent of the Senate and House of Commons, to make Laws for the Peace, Order, and good Government of Canada, in relation to all Matters not coming within the Classes of Subjects by this Act assigned exclusively to the Legislatures of the Provinces; and for greater Certainty, but not so as to restrict the Generality of the foregoing Terms of this Section, it is hereby declared that (notwithstanding anything in this Act) the exclusive Legislative Authority of the Parliament of Canada extends to all Matters coming within the Classes of Subjects next herein-after enumerated; . . .

92. In each Province the Legislature may exclusively make Laws in relation to Matters coming within the Classes of Subjects next herein-after enumerated; that is to say,—

1. The Amendment from Time to Time, notwithstanding anything in this Act, of the Constitution of the Province, except as regards the Office of Lieutenant Governor.

2. Direct Taxation within the Province in order to the raising of a Revenue for Provincial Purposes.

3. The borrowing of Money on the sole Credit of the Province.

4. The Establishment and Tenure of Provincial Offices and the Appointment and Payment of Provincial Officers.

5. The Management and Sale of the Public Lands belonging to the Province and of the Timber and Wood thereon.

6. The Establishment, Maintenance, and Management of Public and Reformatory Prisons in and for the Province.

7. The Establishment, Maintenance, and Management of Hospitals, Asylums, Charities, and Eleemosynary Institutions in and for the Province, other than Marine Hospitals.

8. Municipal Institutions in the Province.

9. Shop, Saloon, Tavern, Auctioneer, and other Licenses in order to the raising of a Revenue for Provincial, Local, or Municipal Purposes.

10. Local Works and Undertakings other than such as are of the following Classes:—

(a) Lines of Steam or other Ships, Railways, Canals, Telegraphs, and other Works and Undertakings connecting the Province with any other or others of the Provinces, or extending beyond the Limits of the Province;

(b) Lines of Steam Ships between the Province and any British or Foreign Country;

(c) Such Works as, although wholly situate within the Province, are before or after their Execution declared by the Parliament of Canada to be for the general Advantage of Canada or for the Advantage of Two or more of the Provinces.

11. The Incorporation of Companies with Provincial Objects.

12. The Solemnization of Marriage in the Province.

13. Property and Civil Rights in the Province.

14. The Administration of Justice in the Province, including the Constitution, Maintenance, and Organization of Provincial Courts, both of Civil and of Criminal Juris-

diction, and including Procedure in Civil Matters in those Courts.

15. The Imposition of Punishment by Fine, Penalty, or Imprisonment for enforcing any Law of the Province made in relation to any Matter coming within any of the Classes of Subjects enumerated in this Section.

16. Generally all Matters of a merely local or private Nature in the Province. . . .

— 30 —

THE TREATY OF WASHINGTON, MAY 8, 1871 [32]

In 1870 a great many problems involving Canada, Great Britain, and the United States required solution. The United States was seeking compensation for damage done by the Alabama, *while Canada held claims against the United States for losses suffered in the Fenian raids. In addition, when the United States abrogated the Reciprocity Treaty, American fishermen lost their right to fish inside the three mile limit in Canadian waters. Canadian efforts to police the waters brought protests from the United States State Department. The navigation of rivers and lakes and the San Juan water boundary also were causes of dispute. When a Joint High Commission met in Washington in 1871 to consider these various differences, the British Colonial Office invited the Canadian Prime Minister, Sir John A. Macdonald, to serve as Commissioner for Canada, the first time a Canadian had served on such a body. The terms finally arrived at and incorporated into the Treaty of Washington left much to be desired as far as Canada was concerned.*

[32] *Treaties and Agreements affecting Canada . . . 1814-1925* (Ottawa, 1927), 37-38, 43-45, 47, 49.

ARTICLE I. Whereas differences have arisen between the Government of the United States and the Government of Her Britannic Majesty, and still exist, growing out of the Acts committed by the several vessels which have given rise to the claims generically known as the *Alabama* claims: . . .

Now, in order to remove and adjust all complaints and claims on the part of the United States, and to provide for the speedy settlement of such claims, which are not admitted by Her Britannic Majesty's Government, the High Contracting Parties agree that all the said claims, growing out of Acts committed by the aforesaid vessels, and generically known as the *Alabama* Claims, shall be referred to a tribunal of arbitration to be composed of five arbitrators to be appointed in the following manner, that is to say: one shall be named by Her Britannic Majesty; one shall be named by the President of the United States; His Majesty the King of Italy shall be requested to name one; the President of the Swiss Confederation shall be requested to name one; and His Majesty the Emperor of Brazil shall be requested to name one. . . .

XVIII. It is agreed by the High Contracting Parties, that, in addition to the liberty secured to the United States' fishermen by the Convention between Great Britain and the United States, signed at London on the 20th day of October, 1818, of taking, curing, and drying fish on certain coasts of the British North American Colonies therein defined, the inhabitants of the United States shall have, in common with the subjects of Her Britannic Majesty, the liberty, for the term of years mentioned in Article XXXIII of this Treaty, to take fish of every kind, except shell-fish, on the seacoasts and shores, and in the bays, harbours, and creeks of the Provinces of Quebec, Nova Scotia and New Brunswick, and the Colony of Prince Edward's Island, and of the several islands thereunto adjacent without being restricted to any distance from the shore, with permission to land upon the said coasts, and shores, and islands, and also upon the Magdalen Islands, for the purpose of drying their nets, and curing their fish; provided that, in so doing, they do not interfere with the rights of private property, or with British fishermen, in the peaceable use of any part of the said coasts in their occupancy for the same purpose.

It is understood that the above-mentioned liberty applies solely to the sea fishery, and that the salmon and shad fisheries, and all other fisheries in rivers and the mouths of rivers are hereby reserved exclusively for British fishermen.

XIX. It is agreed by the High Contracting Parties that British subjects shall have, in common with the citizens of the United States, the liberty, for the term of years mentioned in Article XXXIII of this Treaty, to take fish of every kind, except shell-fish, on the eastern sea-coasts and shores of the United States north of the 39th parallel of north latitude, and on the shores of the several islands thereunto adjacent, and in the bays, harbours, and creeks of the said sea-coasts and shores of the United States and of the said islands, without being restricted to any distance from the shore, with permission to land upon the said coasts of the United States and of the islands aforesaid, for the purpose of drying their nets and curing their fish; provided that, in so doing, they do not interfere with the rights of private property, or with the fishermen of the United States, in the peaceable use of any part of the said coasts in their occupancy for the same purpose.

It is understood that the above-mentioned liberty applies solely to the sea fishery, and that salmon and shad fisheries, and all other fisheries in rivers and mouths of rivers are hereby reserved exclusively for fishermen of the United States. . . .

XXI. It is agreed that, for the term of years mentioned in Article XXXIII of this Treaty, fish-oil and fish of all kinds (except fish of the inland lakes, and the rivers falling into them, and except fish preserved in oil), being the produce of the fisheries of the Dominion of Canada, or of Prince Edward's Island, or of the United States, shall be admitted into each country respectively, free of duty.

XXII. Inasmuch as it is asserted by the Government of Her Britannic Majesty that the privileges accorded to the citizens of the United States under Article XVIII of this Treaty are of greater value than those accorded by

Articles XIX and XXI of this Treaty to the subjects of Her Britannic Majesty, and this assertion is not admitted by the Government of the United States; it is further agreed that Commissioners shall be appointed to determine, having regard to the privileges accorded by the United States to the subjects of Her Britannic Majesty, as stated in Articles XIX and XXI of this Treaty, the amount of any compensation which, in their opinion, ought to be paid by the Government of the United States to the Government of Her Britannic Majesty in return for the privileges accorded to the citizens of the United States under Article XVIII of this Treaty; and that any sum of money which the Commissioners may so award shall be paid by the United States' Government, in a gross sum, within twelve months after such award shall have been given. . . .

XXVI. The navigation of the River St. Lawrence, ascending and descending from the 45th parallel of north latitude, where it ceases to form the boundary between the two countries, from, to, and into the sea, shall forever remain free and open for the purposes of commerce to the citizens of the United States, subject to any laws and regulations of Great Britain or of the Dominion of Canada, not inconsistent with such privilege of free navigation.

The navigation of the Rivers Yukon, Porcupine, and Stikine, ascending and descending from, to, and into the sea, shall forever remain free and open for the purposes of commerce to the subjects of Her Britannic Majesty and to the citizens of the United States, subject to any laws and regulations of either country within its own territory, not inconsistent with such privilege of free navigation. . . .

XXXIII. The foregoing Articles XVIII to XXV inclusive, and Article XXX of this Treaty, shall take effect as soon as the laws required to carry them into operation shall have been passed by the Imperial Parliament of Great Britain, by the Parliament of Canada, and by the Legislature of Prince Edward's Island, on the one hand, and by the Congress of the United States on the other. Such assent having been given, the said Articles shall remain in force for the period of ten years from the date at which they may come into operation, and further, until the expiration of two years after either of the High Contracting Parties shall have given notice to the other of its wish to terminate the same; each of the High Contracting Parties being at liberty to give such notice to the other at the end of the said period of ten years or at any time afterward. . . .

Done in duplicate at Washington, the 8th day of May, in the year of Our Lord, 1871.

(L.S.) DE GREY & RIPON
(L.S.) STAFFORD H. NORTHCOTE
(L.S.) EDWD. THORNTON
(L.S.) JOHN A. MACDONALD
(L.S.) MOUNTAGUE BERNARD
(L.S.) HAMILTON FISH
(L.S.) ROBT. C. SCHENCK
(L.S.) SAMUEL NELSON
(L.S.) EBENEZER ROCKWOOD HOAR
(L.S.) GEO. H. WILLIAMS

— 31 —

THE "NATIONAL POLICY," 1878 [33]

The Liberal party had a tradition of supporting the principle of free trade. When the Mackenzie Liberal ministry replaced that of Sir John A. Macdonald in 1873, as a result of the "Pacific Scandal," the new government tried to establish reciprocal free trade with the United States. The United States Congress, however, was not interested, leaving the way open for Macdonald to counter with a policy of protection. Since the word "protection" was unpopular in some sections of the country, the

[33] *Debates of the House of Commons . . . ,* vol. IV (Ottawa, 1878), I, 854, 1071.

Liberal-Conservative party hit on the happy phrase "Na-
tional Policy" to describe their protectionist views. Mac-
donald himself introduced the programme as an amend-
ment in the budget debate, March 7, 1878. On March 12
the amendment was defeated, but the Liberal-Conservative
party had declared its principles for the future.

✓   ✓   ✓

I move: That the Speaker do not now leave the Chair,
but that this House is of the opinion that the welfare of
Canada requires the adoption of a National Policy, which,
by a judicious readjustment of the Tariff, will benefit and
foster the agricultural, the mining, the manufacturing and
other interests of the Dominion; that such a policy will
retain in Canada thousands of our fellow countrymen now
obliged to expatriate themselves in search of the employment denied them at home, will restore prosperity to our
struggling industries, now so sadly depressed, will prevent
Canada from being made a sacrifice market, will encourage and develop an active interprovincial trade, and
moving (as it ought to do) in the direction of a reciprocity
of tariffs with our neighbours, so far as the varied interests of Canada may demand, will greatly tend to procure
for this country, eventually, a reciprocity of trade.

— 32 —

THE CANADIAN PACIFIC RAILWAY, OCTOBER 21, 1880 [34]

One of the terms under which British Columbia en-
tered Canadian Confederation in 1871 was that Canada
would begin within two years to build a railway to the

[34] *Debates of the House of Commons . . . , vol. X (Ottawa,*
1881), I, 28-31.

*Pacific, and would complete it within ten. The first char-
ter was awarded in 1873 to the Canadian Pacific Railway,
which ran into difficulties over the so-called "Pacific
Scandal." Little was done until the Liberal-Conservative
party, led by Macdonald, returned to power in 1878. A
new contract with a new group of railwaymen was presented to the House of Commons on December 10, 1880.
Extracts from the contract are given below. After almost
insuperable financial and engineering difficulties the line
was completed on November 7, 1885, when the last spike
was driven at Craigellachie in the Rocky Mountains. The
first through train on the system left Montreal at 8 P.M.,
June 28, 1886, and arrived at Port Moody near Vancouver on time, 135 hours later. The young and tenuous
nation had been drawn together.*

    ✓   ✓   ✓

. . . 7. The Railway constructed under the terms hereof
shall be the property of the Company: and pending the
completion of the Eastern and Central sections, the Government shall transfer to the Company the possession and
right to work and run the several portions of the Canadian Pacific Railway already constructed or as the same
shall be completed. And upon the completion of the Eastern and Central sections, the Government shall convey to
the Company, with a suitable number of station buildings
and with water service (but without equipment), those
portions of the Canadian Pacific Railway constructed or
to be constructed by the Government which shall then be
completed; and upon completion of the remainder of the
portion of railway to be constructed by the Government,
that portion shall also be conveyed to the Company, and
the Canadian Pacific Railway shall become, and be thereafter the absolute property of the Company. And the
Company shall thereafter and forever efficiently maintain,
work and run the Canadian Pacific Railway.

8. Upon the reception from the Government of the
possession of each of the respective portions of the Canadian Pacific Railway, the Company shall equip the same
in conformity with the standard herein established for
the equipment of the sections hereby contracted for . . .

9. In consideration of the premises, the Government

agree to grant to the Company a subsidy in money of
$25,000,000, and in land of 25,000,000 acres, for which
subsidies the construction of the Canadian Pacific Railway shall be completed and the same shall be equipped,
maintained and operated, the said subsidies respectively
to be paid and granted as the work of construction shall
proceed . . .

10. In further consideration of the premises the Government shall also grant to the Company the lands required for the roadbed of the railway, and for its stations,
station grounds, workshops, dock ground and water frontage at the termini on navigable waters, buildings, yards,
and other appurtenances required for the convenient and
effectual construction and working of the railway, in so
far as such land shall be vested in the Government. And
the Government shall also permit the admission free of
duty, of all steel rails, fish plates and other fastenings,
spikes, bolts and nuts, wire, timber and all material for
bridges, to be used in the original construction of the railway, and of a telegraph line in connection therewith, and
all telegraphic apparatus required for the first equipment
of such telegraph line. And will convey to the Company,
at cost price, with interest, all rails and fastenings bought
in or since the year 1879, and other materials for construction in the possession of or purchased by the Government at a valuation; such rails, fastenings and materials not being required by it for the construction of the
said Lake Superior and Western sections.

11. The grant of land hereby agreed to be made to the
Company, shall be so made in alternate sections of 640
acres each, extending back 24 miles deep, on each side of
the railway, from Winnipeg to Jasper House, in so far as
such lands shall be vested in the Government, the Company receiving the sections bearing uneven numbers. But
should any of such sections consist in a material degree
of land not fairly fit for settlement, the Company shall not
be obliged to receive them as part of such grant, and the
deficiency thereby caused and any further deficiency which
may arise from the insufficient quantity of land along the
said portion of railway, to complete the said 25,000,000
acres, or from the prevalence of lakes and water
stretches in the sections granted (which lakes and water

stretches shall not be computed in the acreage of such sections), shall be made up from other portions to be selected by the Company in the tract known as the Fertile Belt, that is to say the land lying between parallels 49 and 57 degrees of north latitude or elsewhere at the option of the Company by the grant therein of similar alternate sections extending back 24 miles deep on each side of any branch line or lines of railway to be located by the Company, and to be shown on a map or plan thereof deposited with the Minister of Railways; or of any common front line or lines agreed upon between the Government and the Company, the conditions hereinbefore stated as to lands not fairly fit for settlement to be applicable to such additional grants. And the Company may, with the consent of the Government, select in the North-West Territories any tract or tracts of land not taken up as a means of supplying or partially supplying such deficiency. But such grants shall be made only from lands remaining vested in the Government. . . .

13. The Company shall have the right subject to the approval of the Governor in Council to lay out and locate the line of the railway hereby contracted for, as they may see fit, preserving the following terminal points, namely: from Callander station to the point of junction with the Lake Superior section; and from Selkirk to the junction with the Western section at Kamloops by way of the Yellow Head Pass. . . .

15. For 20 years from the date hereof, no line of railway shall be authorised by the Dominion Parliament to be constructed South of the Canadian Pacific Railway, from any point at or near the Canadian Pacific Railway except such line as shall run South West, or to the Westward of South West: nor to within fifteen miles of Latitude 49. And in the establishment of any new Province in the North West Territories, provision shall be made for continuing such prohibition after such establishment until the expiration of the said period.

16. The Canadian Pacific Railway, and all stations and station grounds, workshops, buildings, yards and other property, rolling stock and appurtenances required and used for the construction and working thereof, and the capital stock of the Company shall be forever free from

taxation by the Dominion, or by any Province hereafter to be established or by any Municipal Corporation therein, and the lands of the Company, in the North-West Territories, untill they are either sold or occupied, shall also be free from such taxation for 20 years after the grant thereof from the Crown. . . .

In witness whereof the parties hereto have executed these presents at the City of Ottawa, this twenty-first day of October, 1880.

   (Signed) CHARLES TUPPER,
        Minister of Railways and Canals
    " GEO. STEPHEN
    " DUNCAN McINTYRE
    " J. S. KENNEDY
    " R. B. ANGUS
    " J. J. HILL
        Per pro. Geo. Stephen
    " MORTON, ROSE & Co.
    " KOHN, REINACH & Co.
        By P. Du P. Grenfell

Signed in presence of F. Braun, and
 Seal of the Department hereto
 affixed by Sir Charles Tupper,
 in presence of

   (Signed) F. BRAUN

— 33 —

WILFRID LAURIER ON SIR JOHN A. MACDONALD, JUNE 8, 1891 [35]

Many words have been spoken and written about Sir John A. Macdonald. But the eulogy in the House of Commons two days after his death by his leading opponent and Canada's greatest orator, in French or English, Wilfrid (later Sir Wilfrid) Laurier, still stands as one of the most sympathetic and yet critical judgments of the man.

✓   ✓   ✓

. . . I fully appreciate the intensity of the grief which fills the souls of all those who were the friends and followers of Sir John Macdonald, at the loss of the great leader whose whole life has been so closely identified with their party; a party upon which he has thrown such brilliancy and lustre. We on this side of the House who were his opponents, who did not believe in his policy, nor in his methods of government; we take our full share of their grief—for the loss which they deplore to-day is far and away beyond and above the ordinary compass of party range. It is in every respect a great national loss, for he who is no more was, in many respects, Canada's most illustrious son, and in every sense Canada's foremost citizen and statesman. At the period of life to which Sir John Macdonald had arrived, death, whenever it comes, cannot be said to come unexpected.

Some few months ago, during the turmoil of the late election, when the country was made aware that on a certain day the physical strength of the veteran Premier

[35] *Debates of the House of Commons* . . . , vol. XXXI (Ottawa, 1891), 884-887.

had not been equal to his courage, and that his intense labour for the time being had prostrated his singularly wiry frame, everybody, with the exception, perhaps, of his buoyant self, was painfully anxious lest perhaps the angel of death had touched him with his wing. When, a few days ago in the heat of an angry discussion the news spread in this House, that of a sudden his condition had become alarming, the surging waves of angry discussion were at once hushed, and every one, friend and foe, realized that this time for a certainty the angel of death had appeared and had crossed the threshold of his home. Thus we were not taken by surprise, and although we were prepared for the sad event, yet it is almost impossible to convince the unwilling mind, that it is true, that Sir John Macdonald is no more, that the chair which we now see vacant shall remain forever vacant; that the face so familiar in this Parliament for the last forty years shall be seen no more, and that the voice so well known shall be heard no more, whether in solemn debate or in pleasant and mirthful tones. In fact, the place of Sir John Macdonald in this country was so large and so absorbing, that it is almost impossible to conceive that the political life of this country, the fate of this country, can continue without him. His loss overwhelms us.

For my part, I say with all truth, his loss overwhelms me, and it also overwhelms this Parliament, as if indeed one of the institutions of the land had given way. Sir John Macdonald now belongs to the ages, and it can be said with certainty, that the career which has just been closed is one of the most remarkable careers of this century. It would be premature at this time to attempt to fix or anticipate what will be the final judgment of history upon him; but there were in his career and in his life, features so prominent and so conspicuous that already they shine with a glow which time cannot alter, which even now appear before the eye such as they will appear to the end in history. I think it can be asserted that for the supreme art of governing men, Sir John Macdonald was gifted as few men in any land or in any age were gifted; gifted with the most high of all qualities, qualities which would have made him famous wherever exercised and which would have shone all the more con-

spicuously the larger the theatre. The fact that he could
congregate together elements the most heterogeneous and
blend them into one compact party, and to the end of his
life keep them steadily under his hand, is perhaps altogether unprecedented. The fact that during all those years
he retained unimpaired not only the confidence, but the
devotion—the ardent devotion and affection of his party,
is evidence that beside those higher qualities of statesmanship to which we were the daily witnesses, he was also
endowed with those inner, subtile, undefinable graces of
soul which win and keep the hearts of men. As to his
statesmanship, it is written in the history of Canada. It
may be said without any exaggeration whatever, that the
life of Sir John Macdonald, from the date he entered
Parliament, is the history of Canada, for he was connected
and associated with all the events, all the facts which
brought Canada from the position Canada then occupied
—the position of two small provinces, having nothing in
common but a common allegiance, united by a bond of
paper, and united by nothing else—to the present state of
development which Canada has reached.

Although my political views compel me to say that, in
my judgment, his actions were not always the best that
could have been taken in the interest of Canada, although
my conscience compels me to say that of late he has im-
puted to his opponents motives as to which I must say in
my heart he has misconceived, yet I am only too glad here
to sink these differences, and to remember only the great
services he has performed for our country—to remember
that his actions always displayed great originality of
views, unbounded fertility of resources, a high level of
intellectual conceptions, and, above all, a far-reaching
vision beyond the event of the day, and still higher, per-
meating the whole, a broad patriotism—a devotion to
Canada's welfare, Canada's advancement, and Canada's
glory. The life of a statesman is always an arduous one,
and very often it is an ungrateful one. More often than
otherwise his actions do not mature until he is in his
grave. Not so, however, in the case of Sir John Macdonald. His career has been a singularly fortunate one.
His reverses were few and of short duration. He was fond
of power, and, in my judgment, if I may say so, that may

be the turning point of the judgment of history. He was fond of power, and he never made any secret of it. Many times we have heard him avow it on the floor of this Parliament, and his ambition in this respect was gratified as, perhaps, no other man's ambition ever was.

In my judgment, even the career of William Pitt can hardly compare with that of Sir John Macdonald in this respect; for although William Pitt, moving in a higher sphere, had to deal with problems greater than our problems, yet I doubt if in the intricate management of a party William Pitt had to contend with difficulties equal to those that Sir John Macdonald had to contend with. In his death, too, he seems to have been singularly happy. Twenty years ago I was told by one who at that time was a close personal and political friend of Sir John Macdonald, that in the intimacy of his domestic circle he was fond of repeating that his end would be as the end of Lord Chatham—that he would be carried away from the floor of the Parliament to die. How true that vision into the future was we now know, for we saw him to the last, with enfeebled health and declining strength, struggling on the floor of Parliament until the hand of fate pinned him to his bed to die. And thus to die with his armour on was probably his ambition. . . .

— 34 —

THE SIFTON IMMIGRATION POLICY, 1904 [36]

The Laurier (Liberal) Ministry from 1896 to 1911 is best remembered for its contribution to the opening up of

[36] *Annual Report of the Department of the Interior for the year 1903-1904* (Ottawa, 1905), ix-x, xxix-xxx, xliv.

the Canadian West. Credit for this achievement must go to Sir Clifford Sifton, Minister of the Interior from 1896 to 1905, who was responsible for western settlement. When once the policy of developing immigration had been decided upon, no efforts were spared. A particularly successful campaign using literature printed in English, French, German, Dutch, Norwegian, and Swedish was launched and its success was undeniable. In the year ending June 30, 1903, 128,364 immigrants entered Canada, and in 1904, 130,330. Between 1896 and 1912, inclusive, immigration totalled over two and a half million. The peak came in 1913 with 400,870. The following extract is from the 1903-1904 report of the Department of the Interior, submitted by the Deputy Minister.

Department of the Interior,
Ottawa, November 8, 1904

To the Honourable Clifford Sifton,
Minister of the Interior,
Ottawa.

Sir,— I have the honour to submit the thirty-first annual report of the Department of the Interior for the fiscal year ending June 30, 1904.

The chief functions for which the department was created in 1873 were the survey and administration of the public lands in Manitoba and the North-west Territories, as well as all other lands the ownership of which is vested in the Dominion of Canada. In 1891, the management of immigration was assigned to the Department of the Interior as it was felt that the work of administering the vacant lands of the country was so closely connected with their settlement that it would be in the public interest that the two duties should be entrusted to the one department. These functions are amongst the most important of any of those devolving upon any branch of the government service. In older countries, where the great bulk of the land has passed from the control of the state, the administration of the public domain is necessarily of secondary importance, as compared with the development of other interests. This, however, could not apply to Canada, where most of the lands, especially in the western regions, are still vested in the Crown, and under existing conditions upon the proper disposal of such lands must rest very largely the future building up of the country.

The steady increase in the flow of immigration that has been directed towards this country, the interest aroused amongst United States capitalists as to its possibilities, the attention which the wealth of its agricultural and other natural resources commands to-day in Great Britain, in Europe, and even in some of the most important British colonies, clearly show that Canada has at last emerged from a state of semi-stagnation in which it had remained for so many years, and its future advance, as judged by the remarkable progress of the past few years, must henceforth be by leaps and bounds.

That Canada, however, should be a nation of fifteen or twenty million inhabitants within a comparatively few years—and there are strong grounds for such belief from present indications—is a consummation to be sincerely wished for, but the question of number, desirable as it may be, is not the chief result aimed at by the department. The social character of the people that are being added to our population, and their adaptability to become loyal, prosperous and contented Canadians, is considered to be a matter of far greater moment. In this endeavour, I am glad to say, the department has been highly successful, as a careful analysis of the result of the work, both as regards the number of new arrivals and the desirable classes to which they belong will amply testify. . . .

From the returns submitted, it will be seen that the result of the work has been highly satisfactory. The total arrivals in Canada during the twelve months ending June 30 last, numbered 130,330, or, on an average, over two thousand five hundred settlers have located in the country every week during that period, and are now engaged in the development of its resources. . . .

It is the largest immigration in the history of Canada. While there are no doubt economic conditions underlying the movement of population from one country to another, over which individual or corporate action has little effect, still, when it is borne in mind that only a few years ago, as evidenced by the returns of that time, Canada was almost ignored by the emigrating world as a field for settlement, and that immediately following the adoption of certain methods for fostering and stimulating British and United States immigration, the number of arrivals from those countries has assumed such large proportions to-day that it exceeds the entire British emigration to the United States, there would appear to be little doubt that to the work of the department and to that alone must be attributed the favourable change that has been brought about. It is true that the country has made a remarkable advance since the flow of British and American immigration first set in, and to the development of the western portion of Canada by a large additional population must be attributed the increased prosperity of the past few years. The same opportunities, however, were available many previous years to incoming settlers as are offered now; the agricultural lands of the public domain were no less productive than they are found to be now by the thousands of well-to-do immigrants who have had the good fortune to take them up as a free gift from the government; railway facilities from ocean to ocean, through the fertile wheat fields of western Canada were afforded as far back as 1887; the gates of Canada, both along the three thousand miles of boundary on the south and at ocean ports, had always been left wide open; the natural resources of the country had always existed, but notwithstanding these favourable conditions, the British settler passed our door on his way to the neighbouring Republic, while the American agriculturist almost seemed to scorn the limitless fields extending to the north of the Western States. The moment, however, that vigorous steps were taken by the department to attract immigration to this country by judicious advertising and by the adoption of practical methods for educating the agricultural classes of the United Kingdom and the United States as to the possibilities of the country, thousands upon thousands of the most desirable settlers are pouring into Canada, and are becoming contented and prosperous citizens. This is certainly one of the most satisfactory features in the future prospects of the Dominion. It seems so manifest that the change has been brought about wholly and directly through the policy of the department that for the present it would not appear to be in the public interest to depart from the methods heretofore followed in this relation, but rather to increase the scope of this important work by even more persistent and systematic efforts in the same direction. . . .

> I have the honour to be, sir,
> Your obedient servant,
> JAS. A. SMART

— 35 —

THE CREATION OF ALBERTA AND SASKATCHEWAN, 1905 [37]

The increase of population in the Northwest Territories in the last years of the 19th century aroused there a demand for responsible government. In 1897 the Canadian Parliament did grant a form of responsible government while maintaining the territorial status. Finally, on September 1, 1905, the provinces of Alberta and Saskatchewan were set up. The following document is the speech made in the House of Commons on February 21, 1905, by the Prime Minister, Sir Wilfrid Laurier, introducing the necessary Bill. It reveals the high quality of Laurier as a speaker in English and describes fully the problems involved in creating the new provinces. Subsequently, the provisions for education were radically amended. In this speech Laurier repeated an observation then current, that as the 19th century had been the century of the United States, so the 20th would be the century of Canada.

[37] *Debates of the House of Commons, first session, tenth Parliament,* vol. LXIX (Ottawa, 1905), 1421-1457.

Rt. Hon. Sir Wilfrid Laurier (Prime Minister) moved for leave to introduce Bill (No. 69) to establish and provide for the government of the province of Alberta. He said: Mr. Speaker, the Bill which I have now the honour to present is for the admission of another member into the Canadian family of provinces. As the House, no doubt, has noticed, this Bill is to be followed immediately by another for the same purpose, in relation to the Province of Saskatchewan. These two Bills are intimately connected; they form part of the same subject; and, by your leave, Sir, the explanations which I have the honour to give to the House, will apply to both. They will apply likewise to the resolutions which will be introduced as the basis for the financial clauses of these Bills.

It has been observed on the floor of this House, as well as outside of this House, that as the nineteenth century had been the century of the United States, so the twentieth century would be the century of Canada. This opinion has not been deemed extravagant. On this continent and across the waters, it has been accepted as the statement of a truth, beyond controversy. The wonderful development of the United States during the space of scarcely more than one hundred years may well be an incitement to our efforts and ambition. . . . We have proceeded upon different methods. We have been satisfied with slower progress. Our institutions in our own Northwest have been developed by gradual stages, so as to ensure at all times among these new communities law and order, and the restraints and safeguards of the highest civilization.

The time has arrived when we are all agreed, I believe, nay, I feel sure, upon both sides of the House, that another step, and the last, can now be taken to complete the passage of the Northwest Territories from what was once necessary tutelage, into the fulness of the rights which, under our constitution, appertain to provinces. . . .

When we came to consider the problem before us it became very soon apparent to me, at all events, that there were four subjects which dominated all the others; . . .

The first was: How many provinces should be admitted
into the confederation coming from the Northwest Territories—one, or two or more? The next question was: in
whom should be vested the ownership of the public
lands? The third question was: What should be the financial terms to be granted to these new provinces? And the
fourth and not the least important by any means was the
question of the school system which would be introduced
—not introduced because it was introduced long ago, but
should be continued in the Territories. . . .

The area of these two provinces together will be about
550,345 square miles. That is, in our estimation, altogether
too large an area to be made into one single province
according to the size of the other provinces, the largest of
which is British Columbia, and the next largest Quebec,
British Columbia with an area of 372,000 square miles
and Quebec with an area of 351,000 square miles. By
dividing it into two you have two provinces of 275,000
square miles in round numbers, each about the size of the
province of Ontario. . . .

The new provinces shall, as a matter of course, be
represented on the floor of this House, and, until another
election takes place, they shall continue to be represented
as they are to-day. There will be in each province a legislative assembly, of which it is proposed that the number
of members shall be twenty-five.

A question which has given some difficulty to the members of the committee who had the preparation of this
Bill, has been the selection of the capitals of the respective
provinces. As to the capital of the province of Saskatchewan, the difficulty is easily solved, it will be, as it is at
present, Regina. But as to the capital of Alberta, the
selection was not so easy. There were three claimants for
it—Calgary, Red Deer and Edmonton, each of which had
a good claim. We have decided that we would not make
any final selection, leaving the final selection to the province itself. In the meantime, if you look at the map you
will see that Edmonton seems to be the most central point,
and therefore we propose to make Edmonton the capital
for the present.

Beyond this, I have only to say that it is the intention to
have this Bill come into force on July 1, next.

The point being settled as to the number of provinces to be admitted into confederation, the next question is that regarding the public lands. In whom should the ownership of the lands be vested? Should they belong to the provinces or to the Dominion? A strong plea was presented to us on behalf of the provinces. It was represented that as a matter of law and equity, the public lands in these two provinces should belong to their governments. This plea was no doubt suggested by the fact that at the time of confederation, all the parties to the original contract, that is to say, the provinces of Nova Scotia, New Brunswick, Ontario and Quebec, each retained her own lands; and when at a later day the province of British Columbia was admitted to the Dominion, she also retained her lands. But, Sir, the cases are not at all parallel. When the provinces which I have named came into confederation, they were already sovereignties. I use that term, because barring their dependence as colonies they were sovereignties in the sense of having the management of their own affairs. Each had a department of government called the Crown Lands Department, which was entrusted with the power of dealing with those lands either for revenue or for settlement. But the case of these new provinces is not at all similar. They never had the ownership of the lands. Those lands were bought by the Dominion government, and they have remained ever since the property of the Dominion government, and have been administered by the Dominion government. Therefore I say that the two cases are not in any way parallel; they are indeed absolutely different. When the provinces which I have named came into confederation they retained the ownership of their lands; but when the two new provinces come into the Dominion, it cannot be said that they can retain the ownership of their lands, as they never had the ownership.

Therefore, the proposition that in equity and justice these lands belong to the provinces is not tenable. But for my part I would not care, in a question of this importance, to rest the case on a mere abstract proposition. We must view it from the grounds of policy; and from the highest grounds of policy, I think it is advisable that the ownership of these lands should continue to be vested in the

Dominion government. We have precedents for this. This is a case in which we can go to the United States for precedents. They are situated very much as we are regarding the ownership of lands and the establishment of new states. Whenever a new state has been created in the American Union, the Federal government has always retained the ownership and management of the public lands. And when we take the records of our own country, we know that when Manitoba was brought into the Dominion, that province was not given the ownership of her lands but it remained in the Dominion government. . . .

But I frankly admit, and we must all recognize, that the provinces in the west, in being deprived of the public lands, are deprived of a valuable source of income. And in that way they complain that they are put on a footing of inequality as compared with the older provinces of the Dominion. Realizing that fact, it is the duty of parliament to make ample, even generous, provision which will compensate the provinces for the retention of the lands by the Federal government, and I believe that in making this provision we shall have the full support of hon. members whether on one side or on the other.

Now I come to the financial terms which should be given to the new provinces. Our constitution, which is to be found in the British North America Act, contains a very remarkable provision. It contains the provision that out of the Federal treasury there shall be paid to the provinces a large amount of money in the shape of subsidies to assist them in carrying on their business. This, I say, is a very extraordinary provision. It is, I believe, unique. . . . I do not think it is sound, but though in my judgment unsound, it is the duty of everybody in this House and in this country to take confederation as we find it, with its good points and its blemishes, and carry it to the end on the principle on which it is established. Therefore upon this point I believe it is the duty of the Canadian parliament to continue that policy in this instance and make a liberal provision for these two new provinces which we are about to admit into the Canadian family. . . .

Let me now recapitulate to see the minimum each province is to receive. At present, this year, the province is to receive for civil government $50,000; for capitation allowance, $200,000, which is going to increase until the population has reached 800,000 souls. It will receive for debt allowance $405,375, and this year it will receive also for land compensation $375,000; total, $1,030,375, to which sum must be added for five years, $62,500, in order to allow the province to provide for her buildings and public works generally. . . .

I now come to the question of education, and this question is perhaps under existing circumstances the most important of all that we have to deal with. There are evidences not a few coming to us from all directions, that the old passions which such a subject has always aroused are not, unfortunately, buried. . . . The government has been warned, threatened from both sides of this question, from those who believe in separate schools and from those who oppose separate schools. These violent appeals are not a surprise to me, at all events, nor do I believe they are a surprise to anybody. . . .

I am not here to advocate separate schools as an abstract proposition but we have introduced into this Bill the two propositions, that the minority shall have the power to establish their own schools and that they shall have the right to share in the public moneys. It is the law to-day. It is in accord with the constitution, with the British North America Act.

— 36 —

THE INTERNATIONAL JOINT COMMISSION, JANUARY 11, 1909 [38]

Relations between Canada and the United States were frequently strained during the years following Confederation. But by 1909 they had improved so markedly that it became possible for Great Britain and the United States to sign a treaty which, according to an official publication of the Canadian Department of External Affairs, "is, without doubt, unique in the history of the United States and Canada and, indeed, in the conduct of relations between any two independent states." [39] This treaty was the Boundary Waters Treaty of 1909. It was designed to settle in a friendly and informal manner differences and disagreements which were bound to arise between the neighboring nations. This treaty provided for the establishment of The International Joint Commission as the means of implementing this common purpose.

✦   ✦   ✦

His Majesty the King of the United Kingdom of Great Britain and Ireland and of the British Dominions beyond the Seas, Emperor of India, and the United States of America, being equally desirous to prevent disputes regarding the use of boundary waters and to settle all questions which are now pending between the United States and the Dominion of Canada involving the rights, obligations, or interests of either in relation to the other or to the inhabitants of the other, along their common frontier, and to make provision for the adjustment and settlement

---

[38] *Treaties and Agreements affecting Canada . . . 1814-1925* (Ottawa, 1927), 312-318.
[39] *External Affairs*, March, 1951, 90.

of all such questions as may hereafter arise, have resolved to conclude a Treaty in furtherance of these ends, and for that purpose have appointed as their respective Plenipotentiaries.

His Britannic Majesty, the Right Honourable James Bryce, O.M., his Ambassador Extraordinary and Plenipotentiary at Washington; and

The President of the United States of America, Elihu Root, Secretary of State of the United States;

Who, after having communicated to one another their full powers, found in good and due form, have agreed upon the following articles: . . .

ARTICLE 7. The High Contracting Parties agree to establish and maintain an International Joint Commission of the United States and Canada composed of six commissioners, three on the part of the United States appointed by the President thereof, and three on the part of the United Kingdom appointed by His Majesty on the recommendation of the Governor in Council of the Dominion of Canada.

ARTICLE 8. This International Joint Commission shall have jurisdiction over and shall pass upon all cases involving the use or obstruction or diversion of the waters with respect to which under Articles 3 and 4 of this Treaty the approval of this Commission is required, and in passing upon such cases the Commission shall be governed by the following rules and principles which are adopted by the High Contracting Parties for this purpose:

The High Contracting Parties shall have, each on its own side of the boundary, equal and similar rights in the use of the waters hereinbefore defined as boundary waters.

The following order of precedence shall be observed among the various uses enumerated hereinafter for these waters, and no use shall be permitted which tends materially to conflict with or restrain any other use which is given preference over it in this order of precedence:

(1) Uses for domestic and sanitary purposes;
(2) Uses for navigation, including the service of canals for the purposes of navigation;

(3) Uses for power and for irrigation purposes.

The foregoing provisions shall not apply to or disturb any existing uses of boundary waters on either side of the boundary. . . .

The majority of the Commissioners shall have power to render a decision. In case the Commission is evenly divided upon any question or matter presented to it for decision, separate reports shall be made by the Commissioners on each side to their own Government. The High Contracting Parties shall thereupon endeavour to agree upon an adjustment of the question or matter of difference, and if an agreement is reached between them, it shall be reduced to writing in the form of a protocol, and shall be communicated to the Commissioners, who shall take such further proceedings as may be necessary to carry out such agreement.

ARTICLE 9. The High Contracting Parties further agree that any other questions or matters of difference arising between them involving the rights, obligations, or interests of either in relation to the other or to the inhabitants of the other, along the common frontier between the United States and the Dominion of Canada, shall be referred from time to time to the International Joint Commission for examination and report, whenever either the Government of the United States or the Government of the Dominion of Canada shall request that such questions or matters of difference be so referred.

The International Joint Commission is authorized in each case so referred to examine into and report upon the facts and circumstances of the particular questions and matters referred, together with such conclusions and recommendations as may be appropriate, subject, however, to any restrictions or exceptions which may be imposed with respect thereto by the terms of the reference.

Such reports of the Commission shall not be regarded as decisions of the questions or matters so submitted either on the facts or the law, and shall in no way have the character of an arbitral award.

The Commission shall make a joint report to both Governments in all cases in which all or a majority of the Commissioners agree, and in case of disagreement the minority may make a joint report to both Governments, or separate reports to their respective Governments.

In case the Commission is evenly divided upon any question or matter referred to it for report, separate reports shall be made by the Commissioners on each side to their own Government.

ARTICLE 10. Any questions or matters of difference arising between the High Contracting Parties involving the rights, obligations, or interests of the United States or of the Dominion of Canada either in relation to each other or to their respective inhabitants, may be referred for decision to the International Joint Commission by the consent of the two Parties, it being understood that on the part of the United States any such action will be by and with the advice and consent of the Senate, and on the part of His Majesty's Government with the consent of the Governor General in Council. In each case so referred, the said Commission is authorized to examine into and report upon the facts and circumstances of the particular questions and matters referred, together with such conclusions and recommendations as may be appropriate, subject, however, to any restrictions or exceptions which may be imposed with respect thereto by the terms of the reference.

A majority of the said Commission shall have power to render a decision or finding upon any of the questions or matters so referred.

If the said Commission is equally divided or otherwise unable to render a decision or finding as to any questions or matters so referred, it shall be the duty of the Commissioners to make a joint report to both Governments, or separate reports to their respective Governments, showing the different conclusions arrived at with regard to the matters or questions so referred, which questions or matters shall thereupon be referred for decision by the High Contracting Parties to an umpire chosen in accordance with the procedure prescribed in the fourth, fifth, and sixth paragraphs of Article XLV of The Hague Convention for the pacific settlement of international disputes, dated October 18, 1907. Such umpire shall have power to render a final decision with respect to those matters and questions so referred on which the Commission failed to agree. . . .

Done at Washington the 11th day of January, in the year of our Lord one thousand nine hundred and nine.

[L.S.] JAMES BRYCE
[L.S.] ELIHU ROOT

— 37 —

THE DEPARTMENT OF EXTERNAL AFFAIRS, JUNE 1, 1909[40]

By 1909 Canada had reached a status which, the government of the day felt, justified the establishment of a Department of External Affairs. The resolution proposing it was introduced on March 4, 1909, and the Act to create the Department (8-9 Edward VII, c. 13) was assented to on May 19, 1909. It was brought into force from and after June 1, 1909. The resolution and debate introducing the bill reveal the thinking of the time.

✓   ✓   ✓

Hon. Chas. Murphy (Secretary of State) moved that the House go into committee to consider the following proposed resolution :

Resolved, that it is expedient that there should be a department of the civil service of Canada to be called the Department of External Affairs, over which the Secretary of State of Canada shall preside, and that the Governor in Council may appoint an officer to be the deputy head of such department at a salary of $5,000 per annum, and such other officers and clerks as may be

[40] *Debates of the House of Commons . . .* , vol. LXXXIX (Ottawa, 1909), I, 1978-1980.

requisite for the due administration of such department at such salaries as, under the Civil Service Amendment Act, 1908, are appropriate to the divisions and subdivisions of the service to which such officers and clerks may be assigned.

He said: Mr. Speaker, I desire to say that the Bill to be founded on this resolution does not involve any serious constitutional change. It aims merely at an improvement in the administration of that class of public affairs which relate to matters other than those of purely internal concern. As the House is aware the Government of Canada holds all its official communications extending beyond the bounds of the Dominion, whether with the Secretary of State for the Colonies, with the various sister dominions, or with His Majesty's ambassadors to foreign countries, through His Excellency the Governor-General; and I might say for the information of the House that it is not proposed to effect any change in this regard by the legislation that is now proposed.

The House is also, I take it, aware, that despatches bearing on all questions of an external character come through His Excellency the Governor-General. They are by His Excellency referred to the Privy Council and by the Privy Council they are in turn referred to the particular department which is supposed to be specially concerned with the subject matter of the communication. In due course the minister at the head of that department reports on these despatches to the Governor-General in Council and that report, if agreed to by council and approved by His Excellency, is transmitted as the answer of his government. Now, this plan looks simple and in the early days of the Dominion it may have worked satisfactorily. These days however are passed, and with the development of the country and the increase in the number and complexity of its international relations it is felt that the old system is inadequate to meet the existing requirements. Those members of the House who are also members of the Privy Council know that official correspondence does not always lend itself to the simple treatment I have outlined. Sometimes it is difficult to tell at first sight to what department a despatch may relate; sometimes a despatch may relate partly to one department and partly to another or to several departments; and it frequently happens that where despatches of a series are referred to a particular department others of the same series may later on find their way to another department which having no knowledge of the earlier correspondence will be at a loss to decide what shall be done. The government feel that it would be a great advantage if all such communications were sent to a common centre where they could be dealt with according to a uniform system; where there would be a small staff of officials trained in the study of these questions, and where at all times it would be possible to ascertain not only the present position of a question but its history from the very beginning. It is with the object of attaining these results that the present resolution is submitted to the House and that the Bill to be founded upon it later will be introduced.

Mr. R. L. Borden. The Secretary of State has not made one thing manifest to my mind, and that is the most important thing of all: Why is it that the Department of the Secretary of State cannot be the common centre to which the hon. gentleman alludes; why cannot that department do all the work that has been outlined in the very brief remarks of the Secretary of State?

Rt. Hon. Sir Wilfrid Laurier (Prime Minister). The Secretary of State has, I think, given the reasons why it is deemed advisable at this stage of our national development to have a department of external affairs. All governments have found it necessary to have a department whose only business shall be to deal with relations with foreign countries, and in our judgment Canada has reached a period in her history when we should follow the example of other countries in that respect, as, for example, the Commonwealth of Australia. In the Department of the Interior we have a department which deals with interior affairs and we have also a department which deals with Indian Affairs alone, it having been found long ago that the dealings with our aborigines required the attention of one department. So it is in the Department of Marine and Fisheries where we have practically one department dealing with marine affairs and another dealing with questions appertaining to our fisheries. I suggest to my hon. friend (Mr. R. L. Borden) that we have now reached a standard as a nation which necessitates the establishment of a Department of External Affairs. . . .

— 38 —

CANADA AT WAR, 1914[41]

When war broke out in Europe in 1914, Canada, with a population of 7,879,000, had a permanent military force of only 3,000 men and an active militia of only 60,000. Steps were taken immediately to organize a Canadian expeditionary force. Volunteers numbering 35,000 officers and men were quickly assembled for preliminary training at Valcartier, Quebec, thanks largely to the energy and resourcefulness of the Honorable Sam Hughes. The first Canadian contingent, consisting of over 33,000 troops, landed at Plymouth on October 16, 1914. Other divisions followed. When hostilities ended, Canada had enlisted 595,441 men and had equipped and sent overseas 418,052. Up to the end of 1918 casualties among Canadian forces numbered 9,989 officers and 204,397 other ranks, revealing the extent to which Canada's forces had been in action. At the second battle of Ypres, April 22-24, 1915, when the Germans launched their first gas attack, Canadian troops distinguished themselves. The dispatches of Sir John French on that occasion provide some of the finest pages in Canadian military history. The unanimity with which Canadians of all parties entered the war, though bitter differences developed later, is shown by the speech of Sir Wilfrid Laurier, leader of the opposition, at the special

[41] *Debates of the House of Commons* . . . , vol. CXVIII (Ottawa, 1914), 8-9.

*war session of Parliament called on August 18, 1914.
Laurier spoke on August 19.*

✓   ✓   ✓

. . . The gravity of the occasion which has called us
together makes it incumbent upon us even to disregard the
formalities and conventionalities which in ordinary times
the rules of the House, written and unwritten, enjoin as a
wise safeguard against precipitate action, but which, on
such an occasion as this, might impede us in dealing with
the momentous question before us. This session has been
called for the purpose of giving the authority of Parliament and the sanction of law to such measures as have
already been taken by the Government, and any further
measures that may be needed, to insure the defence of
Canada and to give what aid may be in our power to the
mother country in the stupendous struggle which now
confronts her. Speaking for those who sit around me,
speaking for the wide constituencies which we represent
in this House, I hasten to say that to all these measures
we are prepared to give immediate assent. If in what has
been done or in what remains to be done there may be
anything which in our judgment should not be done or
should be differently done, we raise no question, we take
no exception, we offer no criticism, and we shall offer no
criticism so long as there is danger at the front. It is our
duty, more pressing upon us than all other duties, at once,
on this first day of this extraordinary session of the Canadian Parliament, to let Great Britain know, and to let
the friends and foes of Great Britain know, that there is
in Canada but one mind and one heart, and that all Canadians stand behind the mother country, conscious and
proud that she has engaged in this war, not from any
selfish motive, for any purpose of aggrandisement, but to
maintain untarnished the honour of her name, to fulfil
her obligations to her allies, to maintain her treaty obligations, and to save civilization from the unbridled lust of
conquest and domination.

We are British subjects, and to-day we are face to face
with the consequences which are involved in that proud
fact. Long we have enjoyed the benefits of our British
citizenship; to-day it is our duty to accept its responsibil-

ities and its sacrifices. We have long said that when Great Britain is at war we are at war; to-day we realize that Great Britain is at war and that Canada is at war also. Our territory is liable to attack and to invasion. So far as invasion is concerned, I do not see that there is any cause for apprehension, for it seems to me obvious that neither Austria nor Germany, our foes in this war, can command any force able to make an attack so far from their base. But no one pretends that our maritime cities on the Pacific and the Atlantic, are free from the possibility of insult by an audacious corsair, who, descending suddenly upon our shores, might subject them to an insolent raid and decamp with his booty before punishment could reach him. This is not an unfounded dread of danger; this is no mere illusion; it is a real and indeed a proximate danger, since it is a matter of notoriety that both on the Pacific and on the Atlantic there are German cruisers whose mission is to inflict all the injury they can upon our commerce, and even to raid our cities should they find our harbours unguarded. We are aware that the Government has already taken measures, and very appropriately, to guard against this danger. We know that one of our battleships on the Pacific has been seeking the enemy, and if she has not yet engaged him it is because the enemy has eluded her pursuit. . . .

The correspondence brought down yesterday, however, has informed us that the Canadian Government has already taken steps to send a contingent of twenty thousand men or thereabouts to take their place in the firing line. Upon this occasion I owe it to the House and to myself to speak with absolute frankness and candour. This is a subject which has often been an occasion of debate in this House. I have always said, and I repeat it on this occasion, that there is but one mind and one heart in Canada. At other times we may have had different views as to the methods by which we are to serve our country and our empire. More than once I have declared that if England were ever in danger—nay, not only in danger, but if she were ever engaged in such a contest as would put her strength to the test—then it would be the duty of Canada to assist the motherland to the utmost of Canada's ability. . . .

— 39 —

CANADA ON VIMY RIDGE, APRIL 9, 1917 [42]

The capture of Vimy Ridge by Canadian troops on April 9, 1917, during the First World War, marks the finest single achievement of Canadian arms. The royal telegram from King George V, brief as it is, reveals the importance of the operation. The account of the action cannot be better told than in the words of the Vimy Ridge panel in the Memorial Chamber in the Peace Tower in Ottawa.

"Vimy Ridge. During the winter 1916-1917, the Corps reorganized while holding from ECURIE to BULLY GRENAY: an Overseas Ministry and a Headquarters were established in London: in Canada factories poured out munitions of war, but voluntary recruiting declined. Early in Jan. elaborate preparations for the Allied offensive, N. and S. of ARRAS were begun. On 27th March, the artillery bombardment opened; it increased gradually until 9th April when, with the four Divs. in concert and in line on 75,000 yards of front, ECURIE-SOUCHEZ, the Cdn. Corps 100,000 strong, crashed through the German lines, swept over VIMY RIDGE, took the guns in FARBUS and GOULOT WOODS, and covered the southern attack by making THELUS village and LA FOLIE FARM secure. WILLERVAL and GIVENCHY were taken on 13th April, ARLEUX on 28th, the line then ran across the DOUAI plain, for 5,000 yards from near OPPY to BOIS DE L'HIRONDELLE. Canadian casualties in April were 13,477."

✓   ✓   ✓

The whole Empire will rejoice at the news of yester-

[42] *The Canada Year Book, 1936* (Ottawa, 1936), 59.

day's successful operations. Canada will be proud that the taking of the coveted Vimy Ridge has fallen to the lot of her troops. I heartily congratulate you and all who have taken part in this splendid achievement. GEORGE R.I.

— 40 —

THE ORIGIN OF CANADIAN NATIONAL RAILWAYS, 1917[43]

A nation, like an individual, can have too much of a good thing and in 1916 Canada had too many railroads. Three great transcontinental systems, the Canadian Pacific, the Grand Trunk (including the Grand Trunk Pacific Railway and the Grand Trunk Railway, and their several branches) and the Canadian Northern, spanned the country. The last two were developments of the 20th century and they were in financial trouble. Canada had 40,000 miles of railroad for a population of 7,500,000,[44] or in other words, only 185 inhabitants to support each mile of railroad. At the same time the United States had 400 inhabitants per mile of line; the United Kingdom, 2,000; Russia, 4,000. Canada had paid handsomely for her position. The total expenditure in subsidies, proceeds of lands sold, loans outstanding or investment, and guarantees outstanding, totalled $968,451,737, and many square miles of land. The crisis in the Grand Trunk and Canadian Northern forced the government, on July 13, 1916, to set up a royal commission to inquire into railways and

[43] *Report of the Royal Commission to inquire into Railways and Transportation in Canada* (Ottawa, 1917), lxxxv-lxxxviii.
[44] According to the *Report*, x.

*transportation in Canada. The commissioners agreed as
to the necessity for constructive aid to bring the railroads
through the crisis, but differed as to the extent and
method of government help desirable. A. H. Smith, of
New York, brought in the minority report, and Sir Henry
L. Drayton, of Ottawa, and W. M. Acworth, of London,
England, the majority report, which ultimately led to the
organization of the Canadian National Railways as a private company in 1919. The following clauses are from the
Drayton-Acworth report.*

✓   ✓   ✓

. . . We summarize our conclusions and recommendations as follows:—

1. The mileage of Canadian railways is very great in
proportion to the population of the country. It has increased out of proportion to the increase of population.

2. Canada's natural waterways make railways less absolutely necessary than in other countries.

3. The net return is so low as to prove that more railways have been built than can be justified on commercial
grounds under present conditions. . . .

7. The development of Canada justified two transcontinental lines. It did not justify three. The Grand Trunk
and Canadian Northern should have been amalgamated. . . .

11. We recommend that the control both of the Grand
Trunk Pacific and of the Grand Trunk be assumed by the
people of Canada on terms hereafter set out. . . .

17. We recommend that the public take control of the
Canadian Northern Company on terms hereafter set
out. . . .

23. We do not recommend that the Grand Trunk,
Grand Trunk Pacific and Canadian Northern Companies
be allowed to go into the hands of a receiver.

24. We recommend that the control of these three companies be transferred to a new body. . . .

27. Having come to the conclusion that direct ownership and operation by the Government is to be avoided,
and that ownership and operation by a commercial company is not possible, we recommend that a new public
authority, a Board of Trustees be incorporated by Act of

Parliament as the "Dominion Railway Company"; and that the Canadian Northern, Grand Trunk and Grand Trunk Pacific be transferred to this body.

28. We recommend that the Government assume responsibility to the Dominion Railway Company for the interest on the existing securities of the transferred companies.

29. We recommend that the Intercolonial and National Transcontinental be also transferred to the Dominion Railway Company, for reasons which we give hereafter.

30. We recommend that the whole of the Dominion Railways be operated by the Trustees as one united system, on a commercial basis, under their own politically undisturbed management, on account of, and for the benefit of, the people of Canada. . . .

39. We recommend that the question be considered whether Canadian Northern shareholders shall be permitted to retain a moderate proportion of the $60,000,000 shares which they now hold; that the precise proportion, if any, and the relation of that proportion to their share of any future profits of the Dominion Railway Company, be fixed by arbitration.

40. We recommend that the entire share capital of the Grand Trunk, guaranteed, preference and ordinary, be surrendered to the Trustees in exchange for an annuity based on a moderate but substantial proportion of $3,600,-000, the average sum paid as dividend in the last ten years; and that this annuity should increase by 40 or 50 per cent after the first seven years.

41. We recommend that the precise figure be fixed by agreement and that it be left to the directors of the Grand Trunk Company (1) to apportion the annuity among the five classes of Grand Trunk shareholders, and (2) to procure such assents of their shareholders as are legally required to complete the transfer. . . .

43. We recommend the transfer to the Trustees of the National Transcontinental, in order that it may take the place it was built to take as part of a great inter-ocean highway, and because its financial position would be hopeless if it terminated in a dead end at Winnipeg.

44. We recommend the transfer of the Intercolonial. (1) in the interest of the Maritime Provinces to whom

the Intercolonial at present can only give a local service
with no adequate terminals beyond Montreal; (2) in the
interest of the taxpayer who has a right to demand efficient and economical expenditure of his money; (3) in
the interest of the railway staff who will secure the wider
opportunities of a great system. . . .

— 41 —

THE HALIBUT TREATY EPISODE, 1923 [45]

*The advance of Canada to nationhood was made by
many stages. One of the important milestones was the
signing of the Halibut Treaty of 1923. Although the protection of halibut fishing in the Pacific was, by reason of
geography, a purely Canadian problem, up to 1923 any
solution would have been considered a matter for British
negotiation with the United States. The Canadian Government, however, claimed at that time that the negotiations should be carried out by a Canadian plenipotentiary
appointed by the King, on the advice of his Canadian
ministers through the British ministers. The British Government acquiesced after a time, and the Canadian envoy,
Ernest Lapointe, Minister of Marine and Fisheries, alone
negotiated and signed the treaty with the United States.
The significance of this episode in Canadian history was
critically examined by Sir Clifford Sifton in an address
to the Toronto Women's Liberal Association on January
8, 1925.*

[45] *Canada's Constitution and Status, An Address by Sir Clif-
ford Sifton to the Toronto Women's Liberal Association,
January 8, 1925.* Typed ms. in the Library, The Winnipeg
Free Press, 6.

✓   ✓   ✓

. . . In the late Fisheries Treaty with the United States, Mr. Lapointe, a Canadian Minister, was commissioned to act on behalf of His Majesty in the signing of the Treaty at Washington. The British Minister at Washington did not sign. There has been much confusion both here and in England in the press and in Parliament with regard to the nature and effect of this step. What happened was that the Canadian Government requested *the British Government* (not His Majesty) to cause full powers to be given to Mr. Lapointe. The British Government acceded to this request. The commission was issued to Mr. Lapointe by the King on the advice of British Ministers which advice was given at the request of the Canadian Government. In acting under this commission Mr. Lapointe was acting on behalf of His Majesty and His Majesty's Government in England and his action was binding upon the British Government and therefore upon the British Empire.

If the Canadian Government had the right to communicate directly with His Majesty as the British Government has, the Canadian Ministers would have advised His Majesty directly and the Commission to Mr. Lapointe would have issued directly on the advice of the Canadian Ministers, and would doubtless have been limited to action on behalf of His Majesty's Canadian Dominion. In that case British Ministers would have had nothing to do with the matter and would not have been responsible. The British Empire at large would not have been bound. Canadian Ministers have not yet the power to communicate with His Majesty directly and up to the present time cannot advise him except through the British Ministers. . . .

— 42 —

THE ALBERTA NATURAL RESOURCES ACT, 1930[46]

When Manitoba, Saskatchewan, and Alberta entered Confederation the natural resources of the provinces were retained by the federal government and the provinces received a subsidy in lieu of the resources. As early as 1911 Alberta appealed to the Laurier Government for the transfer of the resources, at the same time asking to be permitted to retain the subsidy. The request was repeated to subsequent federal governments and ultimately, while the Union Government was in office from 1917 to 1921, not only the premier of Alberta but the premiers of the other prairie provinces requested the immediate transfer of the resources. Discussions continued to break down on the question of the provinces' surrendering the subsidies. Agreement was finally reached on December 14, 1929, in the case of Alberta and Manitoba, and March 20, 1930, in the case of Saskatchewan. Below are reprinted extracts from the Act transferring the natural resources to Alberta. The Act applying to Manitoba (20-21 George V, c. 29) and the Act applying to Saskatchewan (20-21 George V, c. 41) were similar.

↑   ↑   ↑

. . . 1. In order that the Province may be in the same position as the original Provinces of Confederation are in virtue of section one hundred and nine of the *British North America Act, 1867*, the interest of the Crown in all Crown lands, mines, minerals (precious and base) and royalties derived therefrom within the Province, and all sums due or payable for such lands, mines, minerals or royalties, shall, from and after the coming into force of

[46] 20-21 George V, c. 3. Assented to 30th May, 1930.

this agreement and subject as therein otherwise provided, belong to the Province, subject to any trusts existing in respect thereof, and to any interest other than that of the Crown in the same, and the said lands, mines, minerals and royalties shall be administered by the Province for the purposes thereof, subject, until the Legislature of the Province otherwise provides, to the provisions of any Act of the Parliament of Canada relating to such administration; any payment received by Canada in respect of any such lands, mines, minerals or royalties before the coming into force of this agreement shall continue to belong to Canada whether paid in advance or otherwise, it being the intention that, except as herein otherwise specially provided, Canada shall not be liable to account to the Province for any payment made in respect of any of the said lands, mines, minerals or royalties before the coming into force of this agreement, and that the Province shall not be liable to account to Canada for any such payment made thereafter. . . .

20. In lieu of the provision made by subsection one of section twenty of *The Alberta Act*, Canada will, from and after the date of the coming into force of this agreement, pay to the Province by half-yearly payments in advance, on the first days of January and July in each year, an annual sum based upon the population of the Province as from time to time ascertained by the quinquennial census thereof, as follows:

The sum payable until the population of the said Province reaches eight hundred thousand shall be five hundred and sixty-two thousand five hundred dollars;

Thereafter, until such population reaches one million two hundred thousand, the sum payable shall be seven hundred and fifty thousand dollars;

And thereafter the sum payable shall be one million one hundred and twenty-five thousand dollars. . . .

— 43 —

THE STATUTE OF WESTMINSTER, 1931 [47]

Self-government developed in the British Empire over many years and through much legislation. The final Act which made self-government in the dominions complete was the Statute of Westminster. This Act grew out of the Imperial Conferences of 1926 and 1930. The speech from the throne read when the Parliament at Westminster opened on November 10, 1931, stated, "This measure is designed to make clear the powers of Dominion Parliaments and to promote the spirit of free co-operation amongst the Members of the British Commonwealth of Nations." The Bill was introduced on November 12, and passed in the House of Commons on November 24 and in the House of Lords on December 3. Royal Assent was given on December 11, 1931. The Act is printed here in its entirety except for those sections which do not apply to the Dominion of Canada.

✓   ✓   ✓

An Act to give effect to certain Resolutions passed by Imperial Conferences held in the years 1926 and 1930

[11 December, 1931]

Whereas the delegates of His Majesty's Governments in the United Kingdom, the Dominion of Canada, the Commonwealth of Australia, the Dominion of New Zealand, the Union of South Africa, the Irish Free State and Newfoundland, at Imperial Conferences holden at Westminster in the years of our Lord nineteen hundred and twenty-six and nineteen hundred and thirty did concur in making the declarations and resolutions set forth in the Reports of the said Conferences:

[47] 22 George V, c. 4. Prefix to *Statutes of Canada, 1932* (Ottawa, 1932), v-viii.

And whereas it is meet and proper to set out by way of preamble to this Act that, inasmuch as the Crown is the symbol of the free association of the Members of the British Commonwealth of Nations, and as they are united by a common allegiance to the Crown, it would be in accord with the established constitutional position of all the members of the Commonwealth in relation to one another that any alteration in the law touching the Succession to the Throne or the Royal Style and Titles shall hereafter require the assent as well of the Parliaments of all the Dominions as of the Parliament of the United Kingdom:

And whereas it is in accord with the established constitutional position that no law hereafter made by the Parliament of the United Kingdom shall extend to any of the said Dominions as part of the law of that Dominion otherwise than at the request and with the consent of that Dominion:

And whereas it is necessary for the ratifying, confirming and establishing of certain of the said declarations and resolutions of the said Conferences that a law be made and enacted in due form by authority of the Parliament of the United Kingdom:

And whereas the Dominion of Canada, the Commonwealth of Australia, the Dominion of New Zealand, the Union of South Africa, the Irish Free State and Newfoundland have severally requested and consented to the submission of a measure to the Parliament of the United Kingdom for making such provision with regard to the matters aforesaid as is hereafter in this Act contained:

Now, therefore, be it enacted by the King's most Excellent Majesty by and with the advice and consent of the Lords Spiritual and Temporal, and Commons, in this present Parliament assembled, and by the authority of the same, as follows

1. In this Act the expression 'Dominion' means any of the following Dominions, that is to say, the Dominion of Canada, the Commonwealth of Australia, the Dominion of New Zealand, the Union of South Africa, the Irish Free State and Newfoundland.

2. (1) The Colonial Laws Validity Act, 1865, shall not apply to any law made after the commencement of this Act by the Parliament of a Dominion.

(2) No law and no provision of any law made after the commencement of this Act by the Parliament of a Dominion shall be void or inoperative on the ground that it is repugnant to the Law of England, or to the provision of any existing or future Act of Parliament of the United Kingdom, or to any order, rule or regulation made under any such Act, and the powers of the Parliament of a Dominion shall include the power to repeal or amend any such Act, order, rule or regulation in so far as the same is part of the law of the Dominion.

3. It is hereby declared and enacted that the Parliament of a Dominion has full power to make laws having extra-territorial operation.

4. No Act of Parliament of the United Kingdom passed after the commencement of this Act shall extend, or be deemed to extend, to a Dominion as part of the law of that Dominion, unless it is expressly declared in that Act that that Dominion has requested, and consented to, the enactment thereof.

5. Without prejudice to the generality of the foregoing provisions of this Act, sections seven hundred and thirty-five and seven hundred and thirty-six of the Merchant Shipping Act, 1894, shall be construed as though reference therein to the Legislature of a British Possession did not include reference to the Parliament of a Dominion.

6. Without prejudice to the generality of the foregoing provisions of this Act, section four of the Colonial Courts of Admiralty Act, 1890 (which requires certain laws to be reserved for the signification of Her Majesty's pleasure or to contain a suspending clause), and so much of section seven of that Act as requires the approval of Her Majesty in Council to any rules of court for regulating the practice and procedure of a Colonial Court of Admiralty, shall cease to have effect in any Dominion as from the commencement of this Act.

7. (1) Nothing in this Act shall be deemed to apply to the repeal, amendment or alteration of the British North America Acts, 1867 to 1930, or any order, rule or regulation made thereunder.

(2) The provisions of section two of this Act shall extend to laws made by any of the provinces of Canada

and to the powers of the legislatures of such provinces.

(3) The powers conferred by this Act upon the Parliament of Canada or upon the legislatures of the Provinces shall be restricted to the enactment of laws in relation to matters within the competence of the Parliament of Canada or any of the legislatures of the Provinces, respectively. . . .

11. Notwithstanding anything in the Interpretation Act, 1889, the expression 'Colony' shall not, in any Act of the Parliament of the United Kingdom passed after the commencement of this Act, include a Dominion or any province or State forming part of a Dominion.

12. This Act may be cited as the Statute of Westminster, 1931.

— 44 —

THE BRITISH COMMONWEALTH AIR TRAINING PLAN, DECEMBER 17, 1939 [48]

"The battle of Waterloo, it has been said, was won on the playing fields of Eton. The historian of the War of 1939-45 may, with some justification, record that the air battle of Europe was won on the flying fields of Canada." This statement in as dispassionate a publication as the Canada Year Book[49] *does not exaggerate the significance of the British Commonwealth Air Training Plan, under*

[48] *Agreement relating to Training of Pilots and Aircraft Crews in Canada and their subsequent service between The United Kingdom, Canada, Australia and New Zealand* (Ottawa, 1941), 1, 2, 3, 6, 8.

[49] *The Canada Year Book, 1946* (Ottawa, 1946), 1090.

which over 130,000 aircrew were trained in Canada for service in the Royal Air Force, the Royal Australian Air Force, the Royal Canadian Air Force, and the Royal New Zealand Air Force. The plan had its inception in an agreement signed at Ottawa on December 17, 1939, by representatives of the governments of the United Kingdom, Canada, Australia, and New Zealand. The Royal Canadian Air Force was the general manager of the plan, which practically made Canada a vast aerodrome. The original partnership was to remain in force until March 31, 1943, but before that date a new agreement, greatly enlarging the programme, was signed in Ottawa on June 5, 1942, to run until March 31, 1945.

✦   ✦   ✦

MEMORANDUM OF AGREEMENT BETWEEN THE GOVERN-
MENTS OF THE UNITED KINGDOM, CANADA, AUSTRALIA,
AND NEW ZEALAND, RELATING TO TRAINING OF PILOTS
AND AIRCRAFT CREWS IN CANADA AND THEIR SUBSE-
QUENT SERVICE

1. It is agreed between the Governments of the United Kingdom, Canada, Australia, and New Zealand that there shall be set up in Canada a co-operative air training scheme as set out in this Agreement, and that the personnel so trained shall be allocated in accordance with Articles 14 and 15.

2. This Agreement shall become operative at once and shall remain in force until 31st March, 1943; unless, by agreement between the Governments concerned, it be extended or terminated at an earlier date.

3. The Government of Canada will act as administrator of the scheme for itself and the other Governments concerned, as hereinafter provided, and it is understood that the undertakings given herein by the Government of Canada to the other Governments concerned are respectively subject to the due performance on the part of such Governments of their several undertakings given herein in support of the scheme.

4. The Government of Canada, acting as administrator as aforesaid, will take the measures it considers necessary for the setting up of an organization which, when

fully developed, will be capable of completing the training of the following numbers every four weeks :—

Pilots (elementary flying training) 520
Pilots (service flying training) 544
Observers 340
Wireless operator-air gunners 580

. . . 9. The share of the cost of the scheme to be borne by the Government of the United Kingdom will take the form of contributions in kind, to be delivered at such times and in such numbers as may be required for the efficient carrying out of the scheme in accordance with the programme of development set out . . .

10. The Governments of Canada, Australia and New Zealand agree that costs and expenses paid or incurred by the Government of Canada as administrator of the scheme (exclusive of the contribution in kind and expenses to be made and borne by the Government of the United Kingdom . . .) shall be apportioned between them as follows :—

(a) The Government of Canada will bear the whole costs and expenses of the Initial Training and Elementary Flying Training.

(b) The costs and expenses remaining will be apportioned in the following percentages :—

Canada 80.64
Australia 11.28
New Zealand 8.08

. . . 14. It is agreed that the Government of Canada may, out of the Canadian pupils who complete their training under this scheme, fill vacancies which occur in the Home Defence Squadrons of the Royal Canadian Air Force, provided, however, that the numbers so disposed of shall not exceed the following :—

Pilots .... 136 a year
Air observers .... 34 a year
Wireless operator-air gunners .... 58 a year

All the other pupils, on completion of their training, will be placed at the disposal of the Government of the United

Kingdom, subject to that Government's making the arrangements indicated in Article 15, and bearing liability as provided for in Articles 16 and 17 of this Agreement.

15. The United Kingdom Government undertakes that pupils of Canada, Australia and New Zealand shall, after training is completed, be identified with their respective Dominions, either by the method of organizing Dominion units and formations or in some other way, such methods to be agreed upon with the respective Dominion Governments concerned. The United Kingdom Government will initiate inter-governmental discussions to this end. . . . Done in quintuplicate, at Ottawa, this 17th day of December, 1939.

On behalf of the Government of the United Kingdom

RIVERDALE

On behalf of the Government of Canada
W. L. MACKENZIE KING

On behalf of the Government of Australia
S. M. BRUCE

On behalf of the Government of New Zealand
W. J. JORDAN

— 45 —

DECLARATION BY THE PRIME MINISTER OF CANADA AND THE PRESIDENT OF THE UNITED STATES OF AMERICA REGARDING THE ESTABLISHING OF A PERMANENT JOINT BOARD ON DEFENCE MADE ON AUGUST 18, 1940[50]

War in Europe and the collapse of France caused concern in the United States for the defence of North America. On August 17, 1940, Prime Minister Mackenzie King met President Roosevelt, on the invitation of the latter, at Ogdensburg, New York, to discuss the problems of defence common to both nations. After only one day's discussion the two leaders on August 18 announced the establishment of a Permanent Joint Board on Defence.

✓   ✓   ✓

The Prime Minister and the President have discussed the mutual problems of defence in relation to the safety of Canada and the United States.

It has been agreed that a Permanent Joint Board on Defence shall be set up at once by the two countries.

This Permanent Joint Board on Defence shall commence immediate studies relating to sea, land, and air problems including personnel and material.

It will consider in the broad sense the defence of the north half of the Western Hemisphere.

[50] Canada, *Treaty Series, 1940,* No. 14 (Ottawa, 1941).

The Permanent Joint Board on Defence will consist of four or five members from each country, most of them from the services. It will meet shortly.

— 46 —

CANADA AND THE UNITED NATIONS, APRIL 27, 1945 [51]

Canada welcomed the idea of the United Nations. Though the British dominions were not represented at the Dumbarton Oaks conversations which took place in Washington from August 21 to October 7, 1944, representatives of the Canadian diplomatic mission in Washington, along with representatives of Australia, New Zealand, South Africa, and India, met every day with the United Kingdom delegation. Thus, the Canadian Government was kept informed on the progress of the discussions and was able, in turn, to make its views known to the United Kingdom delegation.

On March 5, 1945, the United States, on its own behalf and on behalf of the three sponsoring powers, China, the Soviet Union, and the United Kingdom, invited Canada to attend a United Nations Conference on International Organization at San Francisco. The Parliament of Canada, after full debate, by an overwhelming majority approved a resolution endorsing the Government's acceptance. The Canadian delegation was made up of representatives from both Houses of Parliament and from both sides of each House. It was considered essential that the

[51] Canada, Department of External Affairs, Conference Series, 1945, No. 2. *Report on the United Nations Conference on International Organization,* held at San Francisco, 25th April-26th June, 1945 (Ottawa, 1945), 10-12.

Conference should be assured "the widest possible meas-
ure of support from the Parliament and people of
Canada." The Government, of course, assumed responsi-
bility for the selection of the delegation and for the deci-
sions agreed upon. On April 27, 1945, W. L. Mackenzie
King, Prime Minister of Canada and chairman of the
Canadian delegation, at the second plenary meeting of the
Conference outlined the approach of the Canadian dele-
gation to the problems of the Conference.

Mr. King said:

The Canadian delegation comes to this Conference with
one central purpose in view. That purpose is to co-operate
as completely as we can with the delegations of other
nations in bringing into being, as soon as possible, a
Charter of world security.

This Conference is meeting at a time without parallel
in the history of human affairs. The present is one of
those moments of transition when an old order is passing
away. As representatives of the United Nations, we are
all here to help lay the foundations of a new world order.
The ends that we seek to serve transcend the limits of race
and the bounds of nationality.

We would do well to seek to match our deliberations to
the rapid movement of events. While the fires of war are
still burning fiercely, the opportunity is given to this Conference to forge and fashion from those fires an instrument for world security. In the execution of this great
task there should be no avoidable delay. It is ours to give
to grief-stricken humanity a hope of which it is in greater
need today than it has ever been before. It is ours to help
to bring into being a world community in which social
security and human welfare will become a part of the
inheritance of mankind.

The support we owe to the fighting forces of the United
Nations must extend beyond the theatres of war. It must
look beyond the end of hostilities. We owe it to all who
have borne the heat of the strife; we owe it to the memory
of those who have given their lives, to do all in our
power to ensure that their services and their sacrifice shall
not have been in vain.

In the past, the sacrifices of human life in war have been commemorated in monuments of stone or bronze. The only memorial worthy of the service and sacrifice of this war is one which will help to secure to peoples everywhere the opportunities of a more abundant life.

Perhaps this great gathering would permit me, as one who represents a country which has such close ties with the United States, to say how deeply Canada felt and will continue to feel the loss of so close a friend and so good a neighbour as President Roosevelt. To many here who enjoyed his friendship, his death was a deeply moving, personal bereavement. To the United States, in its national bereavement, I should like again to express our sympathy.

But the passing of Franklin Roosevelt was more than a loss to neighbouring countries. It is a loss to the whole freedom-loving world. That loss places upon each and every one of us a greater responsibility. If the spirit of Franklin Roosevelt pervades the deliberations of this Conference, its success will be assured. The highest tribute which we of the United Nations can pay to his memory is, by our united efforts, to build a world organization which will express his life's aims and his life's ideals—a system of international co-operation which will banish from the world the threat of war, and the fear of war. To those who have come to this continent from other lands I can express no higher hope for the future of mankind than that out of the instrument we are now fashioning there may develop relations among all nations similar to those which for generations have been the common possession of Canada and the United States.

My I add a further personal reference? All present will join with Mr. Stettinius in the hope he expressed that, before the Conference concludes, Mr. Cordell Hull will be sufficiently restored in health to join in our deliberations. Mr. Hull's name will always be associated with the origins of the world security organization. His years of devoted service to the cause of world freedom, his great political wisdom, his fortitude, at his age, in making the arduous journey to Moscow in 1943, and the large share he has had in shaping the proposals we are now con-

sidering have earned for him an enduring place among
the founders of the United Nations.

The proceedings of this Conference have been greatly
facilitated by the preparatory work already done at Dumbarton Oaks and at Yalta by the inviting powers. We
may all rejoice that the Great Powers have achieved
unified proposals for a world security organization. That
is a great step forward, a mighty contribution already
made toward the establishment and maintenance of world
peace.

The rapid movement of events on the battlefronts and
the heavy demands on all who are represented here at
San Francisco make it most desirable to begin as early
as possible the detailed consideration of the proposals
before the Conference.

It is not the intention of the Canadian delegation to put
forth in plenary session special amendments to the proposals. Our delegation will express its point of view at
an appropriate time and place on specific questions as they
arise. Our sole preoccupation in any amendment which we
may put forward or support at a later stage will be to
help in creating an organization which over the years and
decades to come will be strong enough and flexible enough
to stand any strains to which it may be subjected.

We shall not be guided by considerations of national
pride or prestige and shall not seek to have changes made
for reasons such as these. We recognize the principle
that power and responsibility must go hand in hand and
that international security depends primarily upon the
maintenance of an overwhelming preponderance of power
on the side of peace. Power, however, is not exclusively
concentrated in the hands of any four or five states, and
the Conference should not act on the assumption that it
is. Such a position would not only be contrary to the
facts as they have been demonstrated in the past five
years, but it would also be dangerous to the cause of security itself, for it would foster in many smaller countries
the development of a new type of isolationism, a feeling
that the task of preserving the peace could be left exclusively to Great Powers. Such a habit of thought would
make it difficult for the smaller powers to make their

contribution. Experience has shown that the contribution of smaller powers is not a negligible one, either to the preserving of the peace or to its restoration when peace has been disturbed.

The people of Canada are firm in their resolve to do whatever lies in their power to insure that the world will not be engulfed for a third time by a tidal wave of savagery and despotism. That is why our Parliament overwhelmingly endorsed the acceptance of the invitation to Canada to participate in this Conference. That is why our Parliament accepted the proposals of the inviting powers as a satisfactory general basis for the discussion of the proposed Charter. That is why the delegation from Canada received from Parliament a mandate to use its best endeavours at this Conference to further an agreement to establish a world security organization. The measure of the unanimity of our country is to be found in its delegation to this Conference. The delegates were selected while our Parliament was in session. They were chosen from both Houses and from both sides of each House. They represent all important shades of opinion in Canada.

In conclusion, may I express my firm conviction that the spirit in which we approach the great task of this Conference will determine the measure of its success. It is for each nation to remember that over all nations is humanity. It is for all to remember that justice is the common concern of mankind. The years of war have surely taught the supreme lesson that men and nations should not be made to serve selfish national ends, whether those ends be isolated self-defence or world domination. Nations everywhere must unite to save and to serve humanity.

— 47 —

THE UNION OF NEWFOUNDLAND WITH CANADA, MARCH 31, 1949 [52]

In the 1930's Newfoundland found herself in financial straits owing to the depression. The British Government was asked in 1933 to appoint a royal commission to investigate her problems and to make recommendations. In 1934 the Newfoundland constitution was suspended and a Commission of Government, appointed by the Crown, took office. In 1946 Newfoundland elected a national convention to consider her economic situation and future form of government. Shortly afterwards a delegation from the national convention visited Ottawa to discuss federal union of Newfoundland with Canada. Discussions continued for some months. On July 22, 1948, a referendum in Newfoundland favored confederation, in October representatives of Canada and Newfoundland met in Ottawa to discuss final arrangements for Newfoundland's entry into the Dominion, and on December 11, 1948, an agreement was signed. On March 23, 1949, the British North America Act (12-13 George VI, c. 22), passed by the British Parliament for the union of Newfoundland with Canada, received Royal Assent, and on March 31, 1949, Newfoundland became the tenth province of Canada. Following the passing of the British Act, the Canadian Parliament passed an act to approve the terms of union, extracts from which are given below.

ᕗ   ᕗ   ᕗ

His Majesty, by and with the advice and consent of the Senate and House of Commons of Canada, enacts as follows :

[52] 13 George VI, c. 1. Assented to 18th February, 1949.

1. The agreement set out in the Schedule to this Act is hereby approved.

Schedule. . . .
Terms of Union
Union

1. On, from, and after the coming into force of these Terms (hereinafter referred to as the date of Union), Newfoundland shall form part of Canada and shall be a province thereof to be called and known as the Province of Newfoundland.

2. The Province of Newfoundland shall comprise the same territory as at the date of Union, that is to say, the island of Newfoundland and the islands adjacent thereto, the Coast of Labrador as delimited in the report delivered by the Judicial Committee of His Majesty's Privy Council on the first day of March, 1927, and approved by His Majesty in His Privy Council on the twenty-second day of March, 1927, and the islands adjacent to the said Coast of Labrador. . . .

Representation in Parliament

4. The Province of Newfoundland shall be entitled to be represented in the Senate by six members, and in the House of Commons by seven members out of a total membership of two hundred and sixty-two. . . .

Provincial Constitution

7. The Constitution of Newfoundland as it existed immediately prior to the sixteenth day of February, 1934, is revived at the date of Union and shall, subject to these Terms and the British North America Acts, 1867 to 1946, continue as the Constitution of the Province of Newfoundland from and after the date of Union, until altered under the authority of the said Acts. . . .

Education

17. In lieu of section ninety-three of the British North America Act, 1867, the following Term shall apply in respect of the Province of Newfoundland:

In and for the Province of Newfoundland the Legislature shall have exclusive authority to make laws in relation to education, but the Legislature will not have authority to make laws prejudicially affecting any right or privilege with respect to denominational schools, common (amalgamated) schools, or denominational colleges, that any class or classes of persons have by law in Newfoundland at the date of Union, and out of public funds of the Province of Newfoundland, provided for education,

(a) all such schools shall receive their share of such funds in accordance with scales determined on a non-discriminatory basis from time to time by the Legislature for all schools then being conducted under authority of the Legislature; and

(b) all such colleges shall receive their share of any grant from time to time voted for all colleges then being conducted under authority of the Legislature, such grant being distributed on a non-discriminatory basis. . . .

Subsidies

26. Canada will pay to the Province of Newfoundland the following subsidies:

(a) an annual subsidy of $180,000 and an annual subsidy equal to 80 cents per head of the population of the Province of Newfoundland (being taken at 325,000 until the first decennial census after the date of Union), subject to be increased to conform to the scale of grants authorized by the British North America Act, 1907, for the local purposes of the Province and the support of its Government and Legislature, but in no year shall sums payable under this paragraph be less than those payable in the first year after the date of Union; and

(b) an additional annual subsidy of $1,100,000 payable for the like purposes as the various fixed annual allowances and subsidies provided by statutes of the Parliament of Canada from time to time for the Provinces of Nova Scotia, New Brunswick, and Prince Edward Island or any of them and in recognition of the special problems of the Province of Newfoundland by reason of geography and its sparse and scattered population. . . .

Transitional Grants

28. (1) In order to facilitate the adjustment of Newfoundland to the status of a province of Canada and the

developme:it by the Province of Newfoundland of reve-
nue-producing services, Canada will pay to the Province
of Newfoundland each year during the first twelve years
after the date of Union a transitional grant as follows,
payment in each year to be made in equal quarterly in-
stalments commencing on the first day of April, namely,

First year	$6,500,000
Sixth year	3,950,000
Twelfth year	350,000

Statute of Westminster

48. From and after the date of Union the Statute
of Westminster, 1931, shall apply to the Province of
Newfoundland as it applies to the other Provinces of
Canada. . . .

Coming into Force

50. These Terms are agreed to subject to their being
approved by the Parliament of Canada and the Government of Newfoundland; shall take effect notwithstanding
the Newfoundland Act, 1933, or any instrument issued
pursuant thereto; and shall come into force immediately
before the expiration of the thirty-first day of March,
1949, if His Majesty has theretofore given His Assent to
an Act of the Parliament of the United Kingdom of Great
Britain and Northern Ireland confirming the same.

Signed in duplicate at Ottawa this eleventh day of December, 1948.

On behalf of Canada:
  LOUIS S. ST. LAURENT
  BROOKE CLAXTON

On behalf of Newfoundland:
  ALBERT J. WALSH
  F. GORDON BRADLEY
  PHILIP GRUCHY
  JOHN B. McEVOY
  JOSEPH R. SMALLWOOD
  G. A. WINTER

— 48 —

NORTH ATLANTIC TREATY, APRIL 4, 1949[53]

*"Fear of subversive communism allied to Soviet might,"
as the Right Honorable Louis St. Laurent said in the
House of Commons on March 28, 1949, was the main-
spring of the developments leading up to the North Atlantic Security Pact. St. Laurent had expressed his fears by
mid-1947. Delegates from Belgium, Canada, France, Luxembourg, the Netherlands, the United Kingdom, and the
United States, met in Washington on July 6, 1948. The
North Atlantic Treaty, signed at Washington on April 4,
1949, resulted from their deliberations. The treaty was
drawn up under Article 51 of the Charter of the United
Nations, which recognizes the inherent right of individual
and collective self-defence. In Parliament the Treaty was
declared to be of "vital importance for the protecting of
Canada, the preservation of peace, and the development of
political, social and economic cooperation among North
Atlantic democracies." On April 29, 1949, when the bill
was voted on, 185 members of all parties agreed to the
motion of approval and none voted against it.*

ʃ   ʃ   ʃ

NORTH ATLANTIC TREATY

The Parties to this Treaty reaffirm their faith in the
purposes and principles of the Charter of the United
Nations and their desire to live in peace with all peoples
and all governments.

They are determined to safeguard the freedom, common
heritage and civilization of their peoples, founded on the
principles of democracy, individual liberty and the rule
of law.

[53] Canada, *Treaty Series 1949*, No. 7 (Ottawa, 1949).

They seek to promote stability and well-being in the North Atlantic area.

They are resolved to unite their efforts for collective defense and for the preservation of peace and security.

They therefore agree to this North Atlantic Treaty:

ARTICLE 1. The Parties undertake, as set forth in the Charter of the United Nations, to settle any international disputes in which they may be involved by peaceful means in such a manner that international peace and security, and justice, are not endangered, and to refrain in their international relations from the threat or use of force in any manner inconsistent with the purposes of the United Nations.

ARTICLE 2. The Parties will contribute toward the further development of peaceful and friendly international relations by strengthening their free institutions, by bringing about a better understanding of the principles upon which these institutions are founded, and by promoting conditions of stability and well-being. They will seek to eliminate conflict in their international economic policies and will encourage economic collaboration between any or all of them.

ARTICLE 3. In order more effectively to achieve the objectives of this Treaty, the Parties, separately and jointly, by means of continuous and effective self-help and mutual aid, will maintain and develop their individual and collective capacity to resist armed attack.

ARTICLE 4. The Parties will consult together whenever, in the opinion of any of them, the territorial integrity, political independence or security of any of the Parties is threatened.

ARTICLE 5. The Parties agree that an armed attack against one or more of them in Europe or North America shall be considered an attack against them all; and consequently they agree that, if such an armed attack occurs, each of them, in exercise of the right of individual or collective self-defense recognized by Article 51 of the Charter of the United Nations, will assist the Party or Parties so attacked by taking forthwith, individually and in concert with the other Parties, such action as it deems necessary, including the use of armed force, to restore and maintain the security of the North Atlantic area.

Any such armed attack and all measures taken as a result thereof shall immediately be reported to the Security Council. Such measures shall be terminated when the Security Council has taken the measures necessary to restore and maintain international peace and security.

ARTICLE 6. For the purpose of Article 5 an armed attack on one or more of the Parties is deemed to include an armed attack on the territory of any of the Parties in Europe or North America, on the Algerian departments of France, on the occupation forces of any Party in Europe, on the islands under the jurisdiction of any Party in the North Atlantic area north of the Tropic of Cancer or on the vessels or aircraft in this area of any of the Parties.

ARTICLE 7. This Treaty does not affect, and shall not be interpreted as affecting, in any way the rights and obligations under the Charter of the Parties which are members of the United Nations, or the primary responsibility of the Security Council for the maintenance of international peace and security.

ARTICLE 8. Each Party declares that none of the international engagements now in force between it and any other of the Parties or any third state is in conflict with the provisions of this Treaty, and undertakes not to enter into any international engagement in conflict with this Treaty.

ARTICLE 9. The Parties hereby establish a council, on which each of them shall be represented, to consider matters concerning the implementation of this Treaty. The council shall be so organized as to be able to meet promptly at any time. The council shall set up such subsidiary bodies as may be necessary; in particular it shall establish immediately a defense committee which shall recommend measures for the implementation of Articles 3 and 5.

ARTICLE 10. The Parties may, by unanimous agreement, invite any other European state in a position to further the principles of this Treaty and to contribute to the security of the North Atlantic area to accede to this Treaty. Any state so invited may become a party to the Treaty by depositing its instrument of accession with the Government of the United States of America. The Government of the United States of America will inform each of the Parties of the deposit of each such instrument of accession.

ARTICLE 11. This Treaty shall be ratified and its provisions carried out by the Parties in accordance with their respective constitutional processes. The instruments of ratification shall be deposited as soon as possible with the Government of the United States of America, which will notify all the other signatories of each deposit. The Treaty shall enter into force between the states which have ratified it as soon as the ratifications of the majority of the signatories, including the ratifications of Belgium, Canada, France, Luxembourg, the Netherlands, the United Kingdom and the United States, have been deposited and shall come into effect with respect to other states on the date of the deposit of their ratifications.

ARTICLE 12. After the Treaty has been in force for ten years, or at any time thereafter, the Parties shall, if any of them so requests, consult together for the purpose of reviewing the Treaty, having regard for the factors then affecting peace and security in the North Atlantic area, including the development of universal as well as regional arrangements under the Charter of the United Nations for the maintenance of international peace and security.

ARTICLE 13. After the Treaty has been in force for twenty years, any Party may cease to be a party one year after its notice of denunciation has been given to the Government of the United States of America, which will inform the Governments of the other Parties of the deposit of each notice of denunciation.

ARTICLE 14. This Treaty, of which the English and French texts are equally authentic, shall be deposited in the archives of the Government of the United States of America. Duly certified copies thereof will be transmitted by that Government to the Governments of the other signatories.

In witness whereof, the undersigned Plenipotentiaries have signed this Treaty.

Done at Washington, the fourth day of April, 1949.

For the Kingdom of Belgium:
P. H. SPAAK
SILVERCRUYS

For Canada:
LESTER B. PEARSON
H. H. WRONG

For the Kingdom of Denmark:
GUSTAV RASMUSSEN
HENRIK KAUFFMANN

For France:
SCHUMAN
H. BONNET

For Iceland:
BJARNI BENEDIKTSSON
THOR THORS

For Italy:
SFORZA
ALBERTO TARCHIANI

For the Grand Duchy of Luxembourg:
JOS. BECH
HUGHES LE GALLAIS

For the Kingdom of the Netherlands:
STIKKER
E. N. VAN KLEFFENS

For the Kingdom of Norway:
HALVARD M. LANGE
WILHELM MUNTHE MORGENSTIERNE

For Portugal:
JOSE CAEIRO DA MATTA
PEDRO THEOTONIO PEREIRA

For the United Kingdom of Great Britain and Northern Ireland:
ERNEST BEVIN
OLIVER FRANKS

For the United States of America:
DEAN ACHESON

— 49 —

ABOLITION OF APPEALS TO THE PRIVY COUNCIL, 1949 [54]

Although the Statute of Westminister of 1931 marked the attainment of Canadian independence from Britain, one vestige of connection remained in the right of appeal from the Supreme Court of Canada to the Privy Council in Great Britain. In the speech from the throne on September 15, 1949, it was announced that a bill would be introduced to amend the Supreme Court Act so that the Supreme Court of Canada would become the final court of appeal for Canada. The Minister of Justice, the Honorable Stuart Garson, in moving second reading, stated that the proposal represented an important step towards complete nationhood, an opinion not supported by the opposition, who held the view that full national status had been recognized without qualification when Canada signed the Treaty of Versailles. The act was assented to on December 10, 1949.

✓   ✓   ✓

. . . 3. Section fifty-four of the said Act is repealed and the following substituted therefor:—

"54. (1) The Supreme Court shall have, hold and exercise exclusive ultimate appellate civil and criminal jurisdiction within and for Canada; and the judgment of the Court shall, in all cases, be final and conclusive.

(2) Notwithstanding any royal prerogative or anything contained in any Act of the Parliament of the United Kingdom or any Act of the Parliament of Canada or any Act of the legislature of any province of Canada or any other statute or law, no appeal lies or shall be

[54] 13 George VI, c. 37. An act to amend the Supreme Court Act.

brought from or in any respect of the judgment of any
court, judge or judicial officer in Canada to any court of
appeal, tribunal or authority by which, in the United
Kingdom, appeals or petitions to His Majesty in Council
may be ordered to be heard.

(3) *The Judicial Committee Act, 1833,* chapter forty-
one of the statutes of the United Kingdom of Great
Britain and Ireland, 1833, and *The Judicial Committee
Act, 1844,* chapter sixty-nine of the statutes of the United
Kingdom of Great Britain and Ireland, 1844, and all
orders, rules or regulations made under the said Acts are
hereby repealed in so far as the same are part of the law
of Canada." . . .

— 50 —

THE MASSEY COMMISSION, 1951[55]

*On April 8, 1949, the Right Honorable Louis St. Lau-
rent tabled an Order in Council, passed that day, setting
up a royal commission on national development in the
arts, letters, and sciences. The feeling was that it was
desirable that the Canadian people should know as much
as possible about their country, its history and traditions;
their national life and common achievements. An additional aim was to give encouragement to those institutions which expressed national feeling and to examine the
federal agencies and activities which contributed to these
ends. The chairman of the commission was the Right
Honorable Vincent Massey, then Chancellor of the Uni-*

[55] *Royal Commission on National Development in the Arts,
Letters and Sciences, 1949-51* (Ottawa, 1951), 273-274,
287-288, 290-291, 293, 303, 305, 331, 355, 358-360, 363, 377.

*versity of Toronto and subsequently Governor-General of
Canada. Many of the recommendations of the commission,
which reported in 1951, have been implemented.*

✓   ✓   ✓

. . . In the following pages will be found a series of
recommendations proposing federal action in certain of
the matters which we have had under review. These, if
accepted, will involve administrative or legislative action,
and the use of public funds, both in capital grants and
in annual outlay. If all our recommendations were accepted, the total figure might in isolation appear substantial; but in comparison with the costs of other activities
of Government, it would be modest, almost insignificant.
. . . We therefore recommend:

a. That the grant of the privilege of radio broadcasting
in Canada continue to be under the control of the National
Government; that the control of the national broadcasting
system continue to be vested in a single body responsible
to Parliament; that the Canadian Broadcasting Corporation as now constituted be that authority and continue to
provide directly by its operations and indirectly by its
control of the operations of others a national radio broadcasting service free from partisan influence.

b. That the present Board of Governors be enlarged
in order to make it more widely representative.

c. That no private radio broadcasting station operate
in Canada as part of a network without the permission of
the Canadian Broadcasting Corporation. . . .

g. That in future the Canadian Broadcasting Corporation refuse all local commercial business for those stations
which it operates directly, except in places where advertising service from private stations is not available.

h. That the Board of Governors of the Canadian
Broadcasting Corporation refuse all commercial programmes not acceptable in content and that they consider
the possibility of eliminating some of the less desirable
commercial programmes now carried, and of replacing
them by programmes more appropriate to Canadian lis-
teners. . . .

j. That in any development of newspaper facsimile
broadcasting in Canada, government control be limited

to the technical control necessary to ensure that broadcasting channels for this purpose are equitably and efficiently assigned. . . .

a. That direction and control of television broadcasting in Canada continue to be vested in the Canadian Broadcasting Corporation. . . .

h. That the Canadian Broadcasting Corporation exercise a strict control over all television stations in Canada in order to avoid excessive commercialism and to encourage Canadian content and the use of Canadian talent. . . .

h. That a National Library be established without delay; that a librarian be appointed as soon as may be expedient; that the National Library Advisory Committee be reconstituted as a board of trustees of the National Library with the Librarian as Chairman ex officio; that the librarian be charged with the direction of the bibliographic centre which shall be responsible through the librarian to the Board of Trustees. . . .

a. That in addition to the help already being given for research and other purposes the Federal Government make annual contributions to support the work of the universities on the basis of the population of each of the provinces of Canada.

b. That these contributions be made after consultation with the government and the universities of each province, to be distributed to each university proportionately to the student enrolment.

c. That these contributions be sufficient to ensure that the work of the universities of Canada may be carried on in accordance with the needs of the nation. . . .

b. (i) That the Federal Government grant annually to the Council for the Arts, Letters, Humanities and Social Sciences recommended in the final chapter of this Report appropriate funds for the establishment and maintenance of an adequate number of scholarships, studentships and bursaries for post-graduate students of Canadian universities in the humanities, the social sciences and law. . . .

c. That a system of fellowships to be known as The Canada Fellowships be established for the encouragement of mature and advanced work in the humanities, the social sciences and law; that these fellowships be administered by the Council for the Arts, Letters, Humanities and Social Sciences recommended in the final chapter of this Report; and that funds be made available for this purpose.

d. That the Federal Government grant annually to the National Research Council and the Council for the Arts, Letters, Humanities and Social Sciences mentioned above, funds to provide exchange scholarships for scholars and graduate students from other countries, particularly those which grant scholarships to Canadians. . . .

h. That there be created a system of grants for persons engaged in the arts and letters (including broadcasting, films and the press) for work and study either in Canada or abroad; that arrangements be made for grants to artists, musicians and men of letters from abroad for study in Canada; that these grants be administered by the Council for the Arts, Letters, Humanities and Social Sciences mentioned above; and that funds be made available for these purposes. . . .

a. That a body be created to be known as the Canada Council for the Encouragement of the Arts, Letters, Humanities and Social Sciences to stimulate and to help voluntary organizations within these fields, to foster Canada's cultural relations abroad, to perform the functions of a national commission for UNESCO, and to devise and administer a system of scholarships as recommended in Chapter XXII. . . .

— 51 —

ROYAL COMMISSION ON CANADA'S ECONOMIC PROSPECTS, NOVEMBER, 1957[56]

On June 17, 1955, the Prime Minister, Louis S. St. Laurent, announced in the House of Commons that the Government had appointed the royal commission on Canada's economic prospects which had been forecast by the Minister of Finance, Mr. Harris, in his budget speech on April 5. The terms of reference of the Commission directed it to examine and report on Canada's economic prospects. In particular, it was directed to study developments in the supply of basic raw materials and energy sources, prospects for growth and change in domestic and external markets, the growth of population in Canada, trends in productivity and living standards, and prospective requirements for industrial and social capital. Mr. Walter Gordon, of Toronto, was chairman of the Commission. The final report was published in November, 1957. The Commission published in addition a series of thirty-three separate studies on specific topics.

✓   ✓   ✓

. . . A Sketch of a Plausible Future

It is time, though, to reveal the outlines of the economic future that we foresee for Canada if our assumptions are realized and if we manage our affairs well. In that light, the few other preliminary comments we should like to make about economic policy may appear to have more content. It seems probable that, over the next twenty-five years, our population will increase to ap-

[56] *Royal Commission on Canada's Economic Prospects, Final Report* (Ottawa, 1957), 10-12.

proximately 27 million. At the same time the labour force
may well double and reach a figure of perhaps 10 million
by 1980. Because of the quickening pace of technological
change, we think that output per man-hour will show a
higher annual increase over the next two or three decades
on the average than it has during any period of com-
parable length in our history. The result of such an increase in our labour force and of the rise in productivity
that we envisage would be a national income in 1980
three times as large as it was in 1955.

There will also be significant changes in the way the
total output is made up. Agricultural production will continue to grow but will form a smaller percentage of the
total. At the same time external demand for our farm
products will be replaced by domestic demand as the principal dynamic determining the growth and changing
structure of Canadian agriculture; and one result will be
that the raising of livestock will become relatively more
important while grain production will relatively decline.
Canadian agriculture should be able to meet the total
demands that will be made on it over the next ten years
without any significant increase in occupied acreage or
any significant intensification of land use. At some point
after that, however, the changes needed to satisfy growing
demand may be of a rather more fundamental kind. This
will be especially true if, towards the end of the period
under consideration, external demand for wheat, which
will probably remain relatively constant for quite some
time, again begins to move upward.

The course of external demand for the products of
Canada's mines and forests will be very different, in our
opinion. It will be strong and buoyant and will lead to a
large expansion of output. There may well be more than
a 50 per cent increase in the production of lead and cop-
per; almost a doubling in the production of nickel and
zinc; a fourfold increase in the production of aluminum;
and more than a fivefold increase in the production of iron
ore. It is probable that the output of newsprint and wood
pulp will double and that there will be a 60 per cent increase in the output of lumber. Proved reserves of the
principal minerals in Canada are already adequate in most
cases to maintain production at the present levels over the

next twenty-five years, and it is probable that new methods of prospecting will lead to the discovery of hitherto unknown deposits which should enable the increased demands that are anticipated to be met. Present timber resources seem adequate to supply the growth there will be in the forest products industry; but the higher cost of cutting less accessible stands will result in greater attention being paid to silviculture and forest management and Canadians will increasingly come to regard their forest resources as a renewable harvest as lustrous and valuable as the gold of the Prairie wheat fields.

We anticipate that the resource industries, including forestry, fishing, mining and electric power, will grow in relative importance in the economy. In 1955 they accounted for approximately 10 per cent of total output. By 1980 that figure may have risen to approximately 15 per cent. In part, this will reflect growth in the production of some minerals such as iron ore, which will be largely exported in unprocessed form. More significantly, perhaps, it will mean that Canada will have become much more self-sufficient in fuels, since the principal resource industries where output is expected to outstrip the output of the economy as a whole are petroleum, natural gas and electric power. The primary manufacturing industries which are based on our natural resources, including, for example, mineral processing and the manufacture of pulp and newsprint, will also grow; but they do not seem likely to occupy a relatively more important place in the economy than they do today. The secondary manufacturing industries, on the other hand, producing chiefly for the domestic market, are likely to increase in relative importance with their output representing perhaps 25 per cent of the total by 1980, instead of the 22 per cent that they account for today. The great growth that we anticipate in the service industries (including the two broad sectors of the economy "transportation, storage and communications" and "trade, finance and private services"), will be more apparent in the employment opportunities they will provide than in their share of total output. In this sector output is extremely difficult to measure. But because we expect productivity in these industries to rise more slowly than in the economy as a whole, their share of total output may not be much larger than it is at present. Their share of the employed civilian labour force, however, may well increase from approximately 34 per cent to approximately 40 per cent. If civilian government and community services are included, the increase would be from 46 per cent to about 55 per cent. This change, together with a decline in agriculture's share of total employment from 15 per cent to, say, 7 per cent, are the most important changes we would expect in the industrial distribution of the labour force.

As the declining relative importance of agriculture and the growth of employment in the service industries would suggest, most of the population increase will accrue to the cities and towns and the character of the country will become more urban. In 1951, 62 per cent of the population lived in metropolitan areas or in other cities, towns or villages with more than a thousand people. By 1980 that proportion may rise to 80 per cent. Over the same period the proportion of the population living in metropolitan and urban areas of more than 100,000 people may rise from 36 per cent to 56 per cent. Not only will population grow faster in urban than in rural areas, it will also be increasingly concentrated in the larger metropolitan centres. By 1980 both Montreal and Toronto may have grown to be cities of between 2.5 million and 3 million, and Vancouver may be a city of almost 1.5 million. The process of urbanization will call for heavy expenditures on housing, streets and highways, schools, hospitals and other facilities of that kind. Expenditures on the various forms of social capital may well total $100 billion or more over the period, without making allowance for price changes.

Twenty-five years from now new capital formation will probably be financed to a greater degree than is true today by the savings of Canadians. Most of the external capital that will still be required will be supplied by United States residents, we should imagine; and United States ownership and control of a number of our largest and fastest-growing industries will be even greater than it is today, unless there is some change in present corporate practices or government policies. Our trade, though it will be a smaller part of our total economic activity, will also be increasingly focussed on the United States; and, in general, the economic relations between the two countries will become even more closely intertwined. Our deficit on current account by 1980 may be no greater in absolute size than it was in 1956; and the net inflow of foreign capital to cover it will be relatively much less than it is at present.

Our increased wealth will be reflected in much higher personal disposable income per capita, which may increase by some 70 per cent over the next twenty-five years. Some of the fruits of increased productivity will be taken in other forms than money. Average weekly hours of work will decline and there will be more leisure. Retirement will ordinarily come earlier than it does today; and, at the other end of the age scale, a higher proportion of young people will defer starting work until they have taken further training at universities and elsewhere. The problem of providing the teachers and educational facilities that will be required is among the most pressing that we face. . . .

— 52 —

THE ST. LAWRENCE SEAWAY, JULY 1, 1958 [57]

On July 1, 1958, an explosion which blasted a temporary dike allowed water to flow into a man-made lake, twenty-five miles long and from one to four miles in width, in the St. Lawrence River. The purposes of the St. Lawrence lake, as it was called, were (1) to provide water for operating generators in a new powerhouse and

[57] *Debates of the House of Commons* (Ottawa, 1952, 1954), I, 1951 second session, 248-249, 260, IV, 1953-4, 4493.

(2) to link with a canal so that ocean-going vessels could sail where the international section of the St. Lawrence rapids had formerly been. The St. Lawrence Seaway and Power Project was virtually completed. The event was officially described as "a splendid example of international achievement wrought by men of good will for a common purpose." Actually, many difficulties beset the inauguration of the project. Though it had been discussed for many years, it was not until the 1950's that progress was made. Some of the difficulties involved were described by Lester B. Pearson, Secretary of State for External Affairs, in the House of Commons on October 22, 1951. The views of the opposition were shown by Mr. Gordon Graydon later on the same day. The ultimate decision of the Canadian Government to build the seaway alone was announced by the Prime Minister, Louis St. Laurent, in the House of Commons on May 6, 1954. There were Canadians who believed that the Canadian determination to "go it alone" was what in the end brought the United States into participation.

¶   ¶   ¶

Hon. L. B. Pearson *(Secretary of State for External Affairs)*: . . . There is one question in our relations with the United States, that of the St. Lawrence seaway, concerning which we have not been able to reach such an agreed solution. We would like to see that seaway built as an international project as a witness to our good neighbourhood and close cooperation. That, however, has not been possible, and the action, or rather the inaction, of the United States congress, which adjourned last Saturday night, shows, I think, that it is not going to be possible to secure agreement with the United States on this matter at an early date. Therefore we are prepared to recommend that this seaway should be built by Canada, and we shall soon request and expect to receive that cooperation from the United States government which it must be remembered is required under the boundary waters treaty.

The following steps remain in fact to be taken before the Canadian development can take place. In Canada, authorizing legislation, as announced in the speech from the throne at the opening of the present session of parliament, is required and will be introduced to provide for the construction of the St. Lawrence seaway and power project, and to provide for an appropriate agency of the federal government to deal with the construction of the seaway. Then an agreement, the terms of which have already been worked out, must be concluded with the government of Ontario for the construction by the Ontario Hydro Electric Power Commission, together with the appropriate authority in the United States, of the power development in the international rapids section of the river, and with respect to the division of costs between power and navigation. There must also be an agreed division of responsibility with the United States agency for the construction of these power development works. Then, although the situation is somewhat different because the international section of the St. Lawrence stops before the Quebec border is reached, steps are being taken to work out an agreement with the province of Quebec covering possible power developments in that province arising out of the Canadian waterways construction.

And, finally, from the point of view of Canadian action, an application by the Ontario authorities for the construction of the power works must be transmitted by the Canadian government to the international joint commission for approval there.

Then, on the United States side, a decision must be made—and I am now talking of the construction of the Canadian seaway—a decision must be made and approved by the president as to what agency in the United States will be responsible for constructing the United States part of the power project in the international section of the St. Lawrence river. That is a complicated problem in which many United States political considerations are no doubt involved, and the solution of the problem may take some time. At least, it cannot I suppose be reached overnight.

Secondly, for United States action, the agency which is to be responsible for the construction of the United States part of the power development must obtain a licence from the United States power commission. The procedure for obtaining such a licence involves public hearings before the commission, to which all interested parties must be given an opportunity to present their views.

And thirdly, for United States action again, an application by the agency responsible for the construction in the United States must be transmitted for approval by the United States government to the international joint commission in conjunction with a similar application by Ontario.

So far as Canadian action is concerned, that part of it which is a responsibility of the federal government will be pressed without any delay. That is all I wish to say this afternoon, Mr. Speaker, though I could say much more, if time permitted, on our relations with our great and friendly neighbour. . . .

Mr. Gordon Graydon (*Peel*): . . . At this stage of the debate I should like to refer, if I may, to one or two matters mentioned by the minister in his speech a few moments ago. I was glad to note that the government had decided to make a start on the St. Lawrence seaway. I have always felt that there were many advantages, Mr. Speaker, in our proceeding with the St. Lawrence seaway as a Canadian project. I am not so sure that all the advantages which have been pointed out in connection with the project being on an international basis have held water. I am satisfied that there is abroad in Canada today an optimism and enthusiasm that this country is able to do great things by itself. I believe that we have never faced a time when we had more pride in what we can do, more pride in our achievements, than we have today. I believe that one of the things that will be of importance in the St. Lawrence seaway is that the people of Canada will feel that at last Canada is tackling the job alone; she can do the job alone, and it will be in her economic interest, as well as in her interest generally, that she do so.

I want to say to the minister that the only pessimistic note he struck was that he seems to feel that perhaps the enterprise is going to get bogged down, at least temporarily, by old-fashioned red tape. I suggest to the minister that all the red tape he mentioned be cut to the best of his ability, because we should not allow this important enterprise of ours, whether it be from the standpoint of power, navigation or defence, to be bound up in red tape at this time.

Right Hon. L. S. St. Laurent (Prime Minister) : Mr. Speaker, if I may have the unanimous consent of the house to revert to motions, I should like to make a short statement about the St. Lawrence seaway project.

Mr. Speaker: Has the Prime Minister leave of the house?

Some hon. Members: Agreed.

Mr. St. Laurent: According to press reports, which have been confirmed to us by the embassy in Washington the Wiley bill which would provide for the establishment of a United States authority to participate in the St. Lawrence seaway project, was passed today by the United States House of Representatives and our own newspapermen in the press gallery have been anxious to have some statement about it from the Minister of Transport (Mr. Chevrier) or from me and have been told that any statement should first be made here in the house.

It is my understanding, Mr. Speaker, that the legislative processes in the United States are such that several steps yet remain to be taken before this bill becomes law.

As hon. members well know, the governments of Canada and the United States have for several decades now made every effort to get the St. Lawrence seaway and power project under way. In the past, several agreements have been negotiated by representatives of both countries, but for one reason or another difficulties have cropped up which prevented these agreements from being brought to fruition.

In view of these perennial difficulties and of the very urgent need for additional hydro-electric power in the province of Ontario, the Canadian government, in 1951, undertook to construct, maintain and operate an uninterrupted deep waterway between lake Erie and the port of Montreal provided arrangements were made for the concurrent development of the power project in the international section of the St. Lawrence river by fully qualified and authorized agencies of Canada and the United States.

It was after this undertaking was made by the Canadian government that the governments of Canada and the United States submitted joint applications to the international joint commission for the development of the international rapids power project. This application was considered and approved by the international joint commission, and the Ontario Hydro-Electric Power Commission and the New York state power authority have been designated by the Canadian and United States governments respectively to do this work.

The undertaking of the Canadian government, in 1951, to construct the whole seaway was given parliamentary sanction when the St. Lawrence Seaway Authority Act was passed. The government's position has not changed since then and we are still prepared to undertake alone the construction of the seaway. However, as I stated in my memorandum of January 9, 1953, to the ambassador of the United States in Canada, the government was and it still is willing to discuss any specific proposal the United States government might wish to put forward once an entity is designated and authorized to proceed with construction of the United States share of the power works and provided that such discussions do not delay either the power or the seaway project.

INDEX

VAN NOSTRA _____ already published